The Folklore of the British Isles
General Editor: Venetia J. Newall

The Folklore
of
Staffordshire

'For my wife, Kate, and sons, Paul and Daniel'

The Folklore of Staffordshire

JON RAVEN

Illustrations by Gay John Galsworthy

B. T. BATSFORD LTD.
LONDON

First published 1978

© Jon Raven, 1978

ISBN 0 7134 0994 0

Photoset by Weatherby Woolnough,
Wellingborough, Northants
Printed and bound by Billing and Sons Ltd.,
London, Guildford and Worcester
for the Publishers
B. T. Batsford Ltd, 4 Fitzhardinge Street,
London WIH 0AH

Contents

Foreword

EVEN BEFORE local-government reorganisation had removed the Black Country from Staffordshire, the county remained predominantly agricultural. But this is not where its chief fame lies. The Potteries, the most notable local centre of a single industry, are the birthplace of products known and emulated throughout the world. Hans Hansen's *European Folk Art* speaks of the finest achievements of English folk art as in pottery, a view which cannot readily be discounted. 'It is,' the writer continues, 'a forceful demonstration that folk art is not limited to peasant communities; far from being crushed by industrial growth, it often drew inspiration from the potential of mechanical methods.'

Readers of this series need no reminder that folklore is to be found in every branch of society, in urban industrial areas as well as in the countryside. The relationship between traditional behaviour and working-class political advancement forms an important study in itself. *The Rigs of Fair*, a recent book written jointly by Jon Raven and Roy Palmer (author of the Warwickshire volume in this series), discusses the Newcastle Wakes. By the mid-nineteenth century the Wakes, formerly local fairs on a grand scale, were in danger of lapsing completely, but the Chief Constable of the time, Isaac Cottrill, encouraged their revival to distract the working class from politics. This was during the Chartist period, when the powers-that-be were much exercised over political unrest among the masses.

The prolongation of the fairs, with their numerous traditional amusements, for many decades is an interesting by-product of these events.

Pottery, the mainstay of industrial society in north Staffordshire, is often used to express social comment. One of the earlier examples was the Slave Emancipation Society's medal, produced by Josiah Wedgwood in large quantities from 1787. Wedgwood, whose advanced ideas led to the establishment of his model factory and village at Etruria, near Stoke-on-Trent, in 1766, was a committee-member of the Society, and the medal, which showed a kneeling, chained slave, bore the motto: 'Am I not a man and a brother?'

The present cult of collecting military paraphernalia stresses the lack of distinction between medals or similar objects as such, and their transformation into quasi-talismans. The process is commonplace, but a particularly interesting parallel occurs in the history of pottery. About four hundred years ago, Roberto Bellarmino, a Tuscan priest later known as Cardinal Bellarmine, was working in the Netherlands. It seems he was an amiable man, but the intensity of his anti-Protestant teaching enraged his Dutch opponents. So-called Bellarmines, stoneware ale-house bottles decorated with a sinister, bearded face, were made in Holland during his lifetime, as a hostile caricature. They were not copied in England until after 1670, but imported examples arrived here much earlier, and between London and Lincolnshire a considerable number have been excavated as witch-bottles – an unusually dramatic example of the talismanic use of a political object.

Though the Dutch Elers family operated a pottery near Burslem at the end of the seventeenth century, Bellarmines do not appear to have been made in Staffordshire, nor, so far as I know, do they feature in the county's witch-bottle finds. The most distinctive local equivalent – though it also occurs elsewhere – is the pottery bird-shaped whistle, built into old chimneys as a guard against evil spirits. The cradles of Staffordshire ware, often given to married couples at this period to promote fertility, were of more positive and obvious significance. Many examples survive, and the custom evidently persisted into Queen Victoria's reign. The idea, though not the form, was probably inspired by *Fecondité* dishes made in seventeenth-century Surrey, showing a prostrate, naked woman with five children.

There is a clearer connection between Bellarmines and Toby Jugs, first made at Burslem in the 1750s. The family likeness is obvious whether the influence was continental Bellarmines or the English versions made by John Dwight at his factory just north of the Thames. In place of the stereotyped, almost satanic portrait of the maligned Cardinal, Staffordshire potters provided the expressive and highly imaginative caricatures for which they were to become famous. Depicting characters as diverse as Toby Filpot, a hard-drinking Yorkshireman, Bluff King Hal, and the Unfrocked Parson, sometimes known as Dr Johnson, these jugs were real expressions of folk art, far removed from the charmless, mass-produced curios sold today as Tobies. Margaret Lambert and Enid Marx, writing in general terms about Staffordshire figures, spoke of 'these little image toys, reflecting ... not only the tastes but also the passing interests, aspirations and views of many generations of ordinary English people'.

Staffordshire-type figures and Toby Jugs in particular were widely copied, often in distant countries. The jugs were made in Sweden, Estonia and central Europe, and Caldas de Rainha in Portugal produced many in the nineteenth century. During the same period the Auerbach factory, in the Russian hinterland south-east of St Petersburg, made them almost throughout its sixty-year existence. A recent Soviet critic, with little perception, described these products as 'of no artistic worth' – presumably because their inspiration is non-Russian.

It is true that folk art must have a base in popular taste, and early Staffordshire pottery fits ideally within this context. But objects which, in the nineteenth-century commercial milieu, were in production for many decades cannot be summarily dismissed, even if copied from an imported pattern. Industrial communities, indeed modern societies generally, incorporate many features which do not originate locally, and to view folk art or folklore in narrow nationalistic terms results in a major failure of understanding. Jon Raven's treatment of the subject arises from no such constricted outlook. He has already won many admirers as a folk singer and folk musicologist, both in person and through his broadcasts. The present volume will ensure that his circle of friends grows wider still.

London University,
June 1977   Venetia Newall

Acknowledgments

My sincere thanks are due to the following individuals, librarians and their staff who have given freely of their time and facilities to answer the many queries and requests that I have made: Michael Billington (Wolverhampton), Dr John Fletcher (Walsall), Roy Palmer (Birmingham), Wesley Perrins (Stourbridge), Eveline Randall (Wolverhampton), Kate Raven (Wolverhampton), Michael Raven (Stafford), Michael Rix (Wolverhampton); and to the Libraries in Birmingham, Bilston, British Museum Reading Room, Burton, Cannock, Dudley, Halesowen, Leek, Newcastle under Lyme, William Salt Library (Stafford), Stoke-on-Trent, Walsall, Wednesbury, West Bromwich, Wolverhampton. A special note of thanks is due to the staff at Wolverhampton Reference Library.

Introduction

STAFFORDSHIRE DIVIDES into three clearly defined regions – the Black Country, the Potteries and the country area in between; the nineteenth- and twentieth-century historians who devoted some of their time to Staffordshire folklore worked within their own regions, so the picture that emerges is one seen through the eyes of a number of unrelated writers.

In the Black Country or South Staffordshire area, G. T. Lawley was the principal collector and author and, without his very considerable efforts, this book would have been much more difficult to write; F. W. Hackwood was also a prolific writer on Black Country affairs, though much of his folklore material was drawn from Lawley's researches. Apart from these two, there were a large number of local historians who included various snippets of folklore in their town histories.

In the Potteries, and the northern part of the County generally, information and authors tend to be thinner on the ground and the only substantial work is a paper researched, written and read by W.

Wells Bladen to the North Staffordshire Field Club. The paper, entitled *The Folklore of Staffordshire chiefly collected at Stone,* was later included in their *Transactions,* Volume 35, 1899-1901. The rest of the picture is filled out from the accounts of local historians and from a variety of historical and contemporary printed and oral accounts.

The third region, centering on Stafford, the County town, takes in the remainder of the County and does not form a unified area in social and economic terms, as do the other two; the wide spread of the towns and villages prevents any overall sense of community in this area. Sources of information for this part are diverse and cannot be identified with the work of any one writer.

The only books that attempt to give an overall picture of Staffordshire folklore are Robert Plot's *The Natural History of Staffordshire* (1686), Stebbing Shaw's *History and Antiquities of Staffordshire* (1798) and C. H. Poole's *The Customs, Superstitions and Legends of Stafford* (c. 1875). The time span of the books is useful for comparing the nature of certain items of folklore at different periods. All three books make valuable contributions to the County's folklore; Plot's work is particularly useful and almost every writer on Staffordshire affairs makes use of it to some extent.

It was the intention of Charlotte Burne, the author of *Shropshire Folklore,* to carry out an exhaustive study of Staffordshire folklore and to this end she arranged a number of meetings with other historians and folklorists but, in the end, time overtook her efforts and the work never really got underway. Thus this book is the first to draw together the many strands of Staffordshire folklore and bring the efforts of earlier writers to the attention of a late twentieth-century readership; in addition to these earlier writings, contemporary folklore also finds a place in this book, as does the folklore of the nineteenth- and twentieth-century urban and industrial areas.

The first five chapters deal essentially with the world of the supernatural. *Ghosts and Graves* is an appropriate subject for the first chapter since it is one of the areas in which contemporary folklore is most active. In a lesser degree the beliefs that affect everyday life still play some part in the modern community; many of the sayings and traditions are widely known and used, even though the narrators sometimes appear to have tongue in cheek.

The Turning Year constitutes the second group and illustrates all those events and customs that take place on specified dates. Many of the customs and activities no longer occur and are simply pieces of historical folklore. In other cases, the events are still celebrated – New Year, May Day, Christmas, etc. – but the surrounding folklore, games and beliefs have been dispensed with. This seasonal folklore is of great interest and particularly so when the subjects are peculiar to the County. Perhaps the best known of these is the Abbots Bromley Horn Dance which, unlike many other seasonal customs, is still performed regularly and is one of the most documented customs in the country, though the experts are still unable to reach agreement regarding the origin and purpose of the dance.

The final group of chapters deal with the humour, pastimes and work of Staffordshire folk during the nineteenth century and, to some extent, in the present day. These chapters contain a fair amount of urban industrial material which has not been previously published in the context of folklore and is derived from nineteenth-century accounts; many are taken from local newspapers, broadsides and other street literature. The humour of the County has proved a hardy survivor and the characters and stories embodied in nineteenth-century humour are still very much alive. Aynuck and Ayli flourish throughout the Black Country, for instance, where they have reigned supreme as the figure-heads of 'the spirit of the region' for more than a hundred years. They reflect the attitudes of Black Country people towards outsiders and permit local folk to have a laugh at their own expense.

The problems of the average working day in the nineteenth century no longer exist, so that much of the folklore associated with work has died a natural death, as have the beliefs and customs generated by the sports and pastimes of the early and mid-nineteenth century.

The south of the County is fortunate in having a Society that reflects the past and present of the region. The Black Country Society is a thriving and unifying force that takes into account the past, present and future of the area; while documenting and preserving the region's history and traditions, it also caters for the development of present-day life and culture, and has a regional political lobby that ensures a say in future developments. The Society's diverse and unique position arises from the very active part taken by its executive and members and the exceptionally broad social spectrum of its membership. Those concerned with the quality of Black Country life find a more-than-adequate mouth-piece in the activities of the Society.

The Potteries can also claim a thriving folk-life force in the activities of the Victoria Theatre at Stoke-on-Trent where, during the last decade, many fine folk-based documentaries and plays have been performed to audiences from diverse social and economic backgrounds. This articulate dissemination of the culture is likely to prove an important influence on the future of folk-life in the Potteries.

Finally a word of thanks to Miss Humphreys, the Reference Librarian at Wolverhampton Central Library, and her staff, who have patiently sifted through a vast number of enquiries on my behalf. Mention has been made in the acknowledgments, but the nature and degree of their help warrants a special note of thanks.

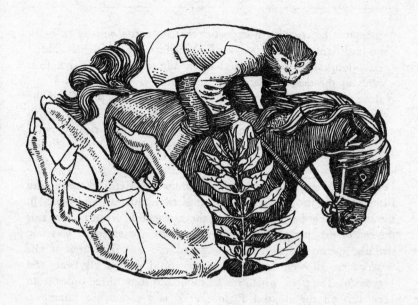

1　Ghosts and Graves

It is clear from the late nineteenth-century 'Notes and Queries'
columns of various Staffordshire newspapers that there was a lively
interest in the supernatural during that period. Thanks to the efforts
of local historians and journalists much of the material was saved for
posterity through their columns, and in the books which they wrote
based on this work. The job of these writers was to report more or
less without comment, whereas their earlier peers sometimes
expressed definite opinions. The seventeenth century produced a
sceptic in Dr Robert Plot, historian and naturalist, whose *Natural
History of Staffordshire* of 1686 has been the source of information to
generations of local historians and folklorists. Terrifying legends were
told of the Black Mere of Morridge: animals would not drink its
waters, birds refused to fly overhead, and a mermaid waited to lure
unsuspecting travellers to certain death. However, Plot commented:

> The water of the Black Mere is not so bad as some have fancied,
> and I take it to be nothing more than such as that in the peat pits,

though it be confidently reported that no cattle will drink of it, no bird light on it, or fly over it; all which are as false as that it is bottomless; it being found upon admeasurement scarce four yards in the deepest place; my horse also drinking, when I was there, as freely of it as ever I saw him in any other place; and the fowls are so far from declining to fly over it that I spoke with several that had seen geese upon it; so that I take this to be as good as the rest, notwithstanding the vulgar disrepute it lies under.

Despite Plot's remarks, the pond, also known as Mermaid's Pool and Blake Mere, continued to inspire speculation and fear, and belief in the mermaid persisted throughout the nineteenth century. Towards the end of that period the waters were partially drained. It was said that the mermaid appeared and warned the workmen that if the waters were allowed to escape they 'would drown all Leek and Leek-Frith'. The pool, which lies in moorland some three miles from Leek, just off the Buxton Road (A53), is a somewhat unprepossessing water-filled hollow, little more than thirty feet in length.

These moorland areas and other similar lonely spots are often connected with ghosts. Various buildings are the haunts of specific named ghosts and there are groups of apparitions warning of death as well as poltergeists, ghosts intended to frighten children, spectres that live in coalmines and make-believe ghosts, the product of local jokes or deliberate deception.

Jack o' the Lantern or Will o' the Wisp, a moorland spirit who also appears in South Staffordshire mines, led men astray:

> Jack o' the Lantern,
> Jack o' the Light,
> Jack in the quagmire
> Every night.
>
> He leads them astray,
> When on their way,
> And leaves them to flounder
> Till break of the day.

Headless horsemen roamed the North Staffordshire moorlands and a terrifying tale is told of the Onecote farmer, who was returning from Leek market at nightfall when he suddenly found himself whirled from the ground and placed on the back of the demon's horse. It sprang forward, leaping fields, hedges and trees effortlessly, until the farmer was flung on the ground close to his home; dazed, battered and maimed, he died several days later. Another man, who caught sight of the ghostly rider, survived but his horse and dog both died. Seven clergymen were called in to exorcise this demon and they forced it to speak. It confessed to being one of the four evil spirits cast out of heaven and forced to roam the earth, till the 'crack of doom' should release it from its lonely wanderings; what the clergymen did with it subsequently is not recorded.

This malevolent apparition is not really typical of Staffordshire. Thus the Kidsgrove boggart does not harm travellers. It is the spirit of a woman murdered in Kidsgrove canal tunnel by the boatman who was transporting her. He was eventually tried and hanged for the murder and, since then, a headless woman has been seen in the woods. Her cries and shrieks caused great terror: they were thought to warn of disaster in the nearby mines.

A few miles further south in the Potteries, a white rabbit would appear in a secluded grove immediately after the terrified voice of a boy had been heard. It simply crossed the path and disappeared; sometimes a cry for help followed. An attempt was made to catch it but the 'hunter' dislocated his shoulder and this caused further alarm in the district. The rabbit appeared near the spot where a murder had been committed. John Holdcroft of Burslem had been strangled by his friend Charles Shaw following a gambling argument. Shaw was tried and sentenced to death in March 1834 but, because of his extreme youth – he was only sixteen years old – the sentence was commuted to transportation for life.

On 21 January 1879, a labouring man was employed to take a cart-load of luggage from Ranton, in Staffordshire, to Woodcote in Shropshire. On his return, at the point where the road crossed the Birmingham and Liverpool canal, an odd black creature with huge white eyes leapt on his horse's back. The man tried to push it off with his whip, but the whip went right through the creature and the carter fell to the ground in fright. The horse, tired from its journey, was strengthened by the 'Thing' on its back and galloped off up the road. Several days later a policeman visited the carter's master in connection with a robbery that had taken place. The man described what had happened to his servant and the policeman commented:

'Oh, was that all, sir? Oh, I know what *that* was. That was the Man-Monkey, sir, as does come again at that bridge ever since the man was drowned in Cut!'

Many Staffordshire spectres, such as the Cornhill Ghost, the Spot Lane (Hilderstone) boggart, and the headless white dog of Leek Brook, have no story attached to them. They are seen in human or animal form, or they may just be noises heard in the undergrowth. A greyhound is said to appear on the Eccleshall Road near Micklow. It comes out from a hedge, walks down the road for some fifty yards, beside and to the right of any late-night traveller, and disappears into a culvert. It was seen by numerous nineteenth-century travellers, but the first occasion was after a Mrs Bratt had committed suicide by drowning in a nearby pit.

Other ghosts haunt particular buildings and their behaviour is as predictable as their appearance, which is often in human form. One particularly interesting story began in 1870 when the mummified arm of a small child and a Cromwellian sword were found in the attic of the White Hart Inn at Caldmore Green, Walsall. The arm was thought to be a relic of witchcraft and became known as 'The Hand of Glory'. This is the traditional name for a charm used by burglars and sorcerers. It was the hand of a hanged felon that was cut from the body as it hung on the gibbet, pickled with various salts, and dried until hard. It was then used as a holder for a candle made of hanged man's fat, virgin wax, and Lapland sesame. Some burglars believed that if the Hand with its lighted candle, were brought into a house at night, none of its sleeping occupants would be able to wake until it was extinguished. The finding of the Hand and sword was related to a legend that the White Hart is haunted by the ghost of a young girl who committed suicide there more than a hundred years ago. A number of licensees reported a variety of strange happenings in the *Walsall Observer* in the 1950s. James Moran, the licensee in 1955, found a hand print on a table in the loft; the print was fairly small, probably that of a woman, though, as far as he knew, no one had been in the loft. Another licensee woke and saw a ghost standing at his bedside. Relief manager, James Paxton, a former RAF policeman, told the *Walsall Observer*:

On Sunday, about two years ago, I was sitting in the living quarters of the Inn – that's the floor below the loft – making up the books. Then I heard the noises. It was like someone slowly pacing the floor of the loft . . . bump, bump. I looked towards the door, which was slightly open. There was one of the inn's dogs, a big Alsatian, standing stiff, its fur bristling, looking up the stairs. That was enough for me. I ran down the stairs as fast as my legs would carry me and nothing would persuade me to go back up there again. No, I wouldn't spend a night in that loft for £1,000.

The arm has been inspected by the Birmingham University Medical School, who reported it to be a hospital or laboratory specimen, skilfully dissected by a surgeon and injected with formalin. In 1962 some members of the South Staffordshire Metaphysical Society spent a night in the attic; though they had nothing unusual to report, they noted that the air in the attic was much colder than that outside. The arm, carefully preserved in a glass case in the Central Library, Walsall, is not on public display, but may be seen by request.

Mysterious bumps, and lights turned on and off, were observed at the Queens Hotel in North Street, Wolverhampton. The licensee, Tony Hipkiss, and his wife told their story to the *Express and Star* in December 1974. The bumping noise, like a door closing, seemed to come from the cellar, where there is a walled up passage-way, and it was suggested that the sounds might have been made by long-dead actors, making their way from the nearby Queens music hall which used to stand in Queens Square. Once, when Mrs Hipkiss was showing friends round the cellar, the lights went on and off repeatedly, though no one was near the light switch.

Some fifteen miles away at the Coach and Horses pub, Great Haywood, near Stafford, staff and customers reported seeing a man in the road; yet, after emergency braking, they found no one when they looked round. A barman, Colin Morrissey, swerved into a ditch to avoid the 'man' and eighteen-year-old customer Jackie Buxton told the *Express and Star* in April 1976 that she was certain she had knocked someone down. An ex-landlord of the pub, Reggie Smith, hanged himself in the loft, and his ghost is said to appear at intervals. It is blamed for gas taps which are turned off in the cellar and pot-plants moving without visible means.

Another spectre is said to walk the rooms and passages of a Stoke-on-Trent pottery. In March of 1967, the *Evening Sentinel* reported a number of 'sightings' of a 'ghost' at the factory of W. T. Copeland in the Potteries. One of the firm's artists, Bill Basford, described his experience to the paper:

> It was some years ago now. I had been playing table tennis in the firm's canteen late at night and one of the lads sent me up to the room to get some table tennis balls.
>
> I climbed the stairs in the old part of the factory. It was dark, but I didn't bother to switch on the light of the room. I just reached in and started to get the balls off a shelf.
>
> Down at the end of the room I saw an old man leaning over a bench as if he was painting. I looked again and he looked up. He had white hair and a moustache and a very white face.
>
> I just ran. There was something terrible about it. . . .

One other employee claims to have seen the ghost, and several others have heard the sound of footsteps in the same area of the factory as that in which Bill Basford saw the old man. Harold Holdway, the firm's art director at the time, heard them when he was working in a dark-room with another person. Both of them rushed out when the footsteps went past their door, but could see nothing. They returned to work and the footsteps started again, moving past their door into the engraving room. The two ran immediately to the engraving room, but found it empty, though the other door to the room was bolted.

Further to the west of the County, near its border with Shropshire, there once stood a moated mansion, built in the reign of Henry VIII. Norbury Manor, as it was called, later became a farm-house and then fell into disuse. In the late eighteenth century it was said to be haunted, but during the second decade of the nineteenth century it was demolished, and the stones were used to build a new farm-house about a hundred yards from the original site. The ghosts, however, moved with the stones and they were often heard at night in the empty rooms and passages. When brewing was in progress, the vessels were put ready for the morning's work. Throughout the night the occupants were troubled by the sound and smell of brewing, but in the morning the equipment was clean and the vessels empty, just as they had been left the night before.

A more macabre story is that of the ghost which haunted Haden Hall at Rowley Regis. It was told by William Green (1834-1924),

whose father had been a gardener on the Haden Hall Estate. Many
years before, a young priest from Hales Abbey had broken his vows
by falling in love with a local girl. One night they resolved to flee
the abbey, through an underground passage leading to Haden Hall.
Unhappily they were caught and, as a punishment, were walled up
alive in the passage. Since then the girl, Elaine, is said to appear near
the Hall, wringing her hands and searching for her lover.

At the same period, in the north of the County, at Hulton Abbey,
a monk named Robert made a pact with the Devil, having failed, as
he thought, to achieve success by conventional means. He longed to
be successful, even though it meant being barred from heaven for a
thousand years. Unknown to him the old Abbot had just been
elevated to York and Monk Robert appointed in his place. The old
man decided to keep the news until Christmas Day and tell it as a
special Christmas gift. The monk, full of ugly thoughts, proceeded
with his pact in order to become 'Lord of Hulton Vale'. When he
learned of his new appointment he was filled with remorse and went
to a holy hermit at Bagnal to seek his advice and, hopefully,
absolution. The hermit admonished him and advised returning to the
Abbey to take up his duties; by properly performing them and
leading a sinless life he would finally escape the Devil, whose
influence would fade. His true punishment would be after death,
when his spirit would wander Hulton Vale for a thousand years
before entering heaven.

A more light-hearted tale connected with a religious house comes
from Uttoxeter in the mid-eastern part of the County. Lady Tansley,
a lady abbess, was crossing from Tutbury to Uttoxeter with a single
attendant. They lost their way, but were able to reach Uttoxeter by
following the sound of the curfew-bell. The abbess was so pleased
that she left a bell full of money, to ensure that it might be rung
perpetually. The strength of the tradition was such that three tangs
were given for the lady abbess night and morning, prior to the
ringing of the curfew bell. Once, it is said, a daring person omitted
the tangs and was greatly alarmed by the sudden appearance of the
abbess, who descended the toll rope and vanished.

Other spectres include the miser of Oulton Vicarage, who returns
each month to count his money, a task which had been interrupted
by his death; Jimmy the butcher's ghost of Bilston who, plagued by
cheeky children when alive, returned to frighten them away from his

house and field – he was finally 'laid' when a railway cutting was driven through his field – and the ghost of a servant-girl, murdered by her mistress, Mrs Hargreaves, who lived near Rushton in the eighteenth century. This last was very striking, for the ghost appeared every night to torment her murderer. It was eventually laid by the reading of Latin – another traditional method – but reappeared as a phantom in the form of a dim blue light, frequently pointed out by coach drivers to their passengers. The majority of these ghosts have not been reported in this century.

There are two dramatic town ghosts – Spring Heel Jack and Molly Lee. Spring Heel Jack was well known throughout the Black Country, and often in the nineteenth century hundreds gathered on the cinder banks when it was thought that he would appear; those who had seen him described how he would leap from roof to roof and steeple to steeple in a ghostly display of aerobatics. Spring Heel Jack also features in the lore of the Midland canal folk. Molly Lee, who had the reputation of being a witch, was an old lady who used to sell milk in Burslem. After death she was said to appear in the streets, complete with milk pail on her head, reciting the couplet:

> Weight and measure sold I never,
> Milk and water sold I ever.

She would also appear in people's homes, where she would sit in a corner, knitting or muttering incantations. She might appear at any time of the day or night and eventually those who were troubled persuaded the clergy to attempt to lay her. Six parsons were brought to Burslem church and a stone pig-trough was placed in the middle of the church. The parsons prayed that her spirit might have rest and eventually she appeared, floating near the roof of the church. Further hard praying brought the spirit to rest in the trough, which was at once placed on her grave. It was said the clergy struggled so hard with the spirit that three died and the others were very ill for some time after.

Perhaps the most unpopular phantoms were those warning of death. They might appear in the form of a tall dark figure, or an animal – a rabbit or large black dog. The Comberford family at

Comberford Hall would hear three knocks; further south in Sedgley, a family was troubled by a huge black dog with eyes like tea cups. The dog would appear before a death in the family. Once it was said to have followed a member of the family home. No sooner had he reached the house than the animal howled. Just then the house collapsed, burying the man in the ruins and killing him. The same incident was reported by a family at Ettingshall Lane, Wolverhampton, some six or seven miles from Sedgley. At Kidsgrove, in the north, from time to time, a white rabbit crossed the Avenue leading to Clough Hall. This was said to predict a death in the family of the person who saw it, and the informant claimed that, three days after he had seen the creature, his father died.

The colliers of the Black Country, in common with many elsewhere, generally believed that any articles stolen from a dead comrade would cause the spirit of the deceased to haunt the mine until the item was restored; this is probably related to the old and widespread custom of going to the grave 'whole', i.e. complete with all bodily parts and possessions. Tildesley, a local historian, recalled being told of an incident involving the theft of a jacket – a particular collier kept seeing the ghost of his dead comrade near him in the mine. Soon after, while working in a lonely part of the mine, he saw the ghost take up the offending jacket, which was lying beside him, put it on and lean against the wall, staring glassily at the thief. After this incident the man confessed and made due reparation to the family of the spirit.

Related to this story is the belief that the spirits of dead miners hover in the pits between the time of their death and the funeral. For this reason, miners commonly refused to work the pits until the funeral of a dead comrade had taken place. The presence of such apparitions and evil spirits in the mines gave rise to 'wise men', who exorcised them. These 'wise men' were often known as white witches. At Bilston, during the late eighteenth century, the local colliers often resorted to the 'White Rabbit', whose real name is not known. On one occasion, when a group of miners had seen an apparition, he was called in to deal with it. He first made various secret signs, and then told the miners that the bravest should visit the pit at midnight, the leader carrying a bible in his right hand and a key in his left. There they were to proceed through the workings repeating the lines:

Matthew, Mark, Luke and John,
God bless the errand we're come on.

They were to follow this by chanting the Lord's Prayer, which was sometimes repeated backwards. As the procession approached the heart of the workings, the apparition appeared. The colliers chanted their lines for all they were worth, but the ghastly form continued to advance unchecked. Just as they were ready to break up and run, one of the men noticed that their leader, nick-named Caggy because he was left-handed, had the Bible in his left hand. The miner called out: 'Caggy yow idiot, put the buik in yer right 'ond.' Caggy quickly transferred the Bible to his right hand and the apparition disappeared, leaving behind a faint smell of brimstone. This method of laying a ghost is different from that practised by most clergymen, as we have seen in the case of Molly Lee, who was laid in a stone trough by six clergymen reading prayers. The same effect might also be achieved by an easier method, suggested by a parishioner to the Reverend Mr Rooker, vicar of St James Church at Lower Gornal, who was troubled by a ghost in 1881:

The idea cannot be dispelled that the church-yard is haunted, and to show the kind of superstition which exists, it may be stated that a few nights ago a woman called at the vicarage and requested the Reverend Mr Rooker to permit her to cut a turf four inches square from a particular grave in the churchyard, in which she alleged was a young man who could not lie at ease in his grave in consequence of a guilty conscience. She stated that if a turf were put under the Communion table, and allowed to remain four days, all ghosts would disappear, and be laid at rest for ever.

Other ghosts were laid by reading Latin and one spirit, the Bradnop ghost, was laid, in the form of a bird, in the cupboard of a house in Leek; the cupboard was then nailed up. No explanation is given of how the spirit was persuaded to enter the bird.

Much less common were the ghosts who specialised in poltergeist activities and those who frightened children. At Hilderstone Manor: 'mysterious noises are heard – moving of furniture, footsteps, doors opening, clock-winding, and general pandemonium. This house is new. The first occupant never heard anything. No death ever happened in the house.' Those interested in the metaphysical see connections between the presence of teenagers in a household and the occurence of poltergeist activities, though the account did not detail the family members at the time of the haunting in the late nineteenth century.

There is a children's ghost in the old rhyme used by parents to frighten children:

> Rawhead and Bloody Bones
> Steals naughty children from their homes,
> Takes them to his dirty den
> And they are never seen again.

Rawhead was said to reside at the bottom of an old pit-shaft. Braver children would shout down one of these shafts, 'Rawhead and Bloody Bones', and then take to their heels.

There are a number of 'ghosts' that haunted particular buildings and were eventually traced to some dubious and illegal project carried out by living people. One such case concerns a father and son, who wished to conceal their counterfeiting activities. They 'haunted' a derelict house at Bilston Brook where they did their coining. People believed that the ghost was an iron puddler, whose head had been blown off in a boiler explosion. Eventually the police heard of the 'ghost' and visited the house, where they caught father and son red-handed. This event took place in the 1830s but similar tales, often quite humourous, were being told during the nineteenth century.

It is clear from the Staffordshire evidence that certain families are connected with ghosts. While the traditional figure in a flowing white gown or the apparition in the shape of an animal are seldom reported today, there are many who claim to have seen or heard ghosts. The story of the young girl who haunted the White Hart Inn at Caldmore Green, Walsall, is one example. The Cacchionnes are a Wolverhampton family with a long history of the supernatural. Joseph Cacchionne, whose parents came over from Italy in the 1870s, was born in Wolverhampton and has lived there all his life. He, his brothers and sisters all claim to have experienced supernatural events, including an apparition seen by his sister, Marie, in the hollow near the waterworks on the Shifnal-Wolverhampton road; a poltergeist experienced by Carl when living at his father's home in the 1920s, and a spirit that came to him in the house of his sister Phyllis; she had it exorcised by a minister. His brother Tony's widow heard a death omen: heavy footsteps in the bedroom. She called up to her husband, who was then alive, but he had gone to town some time before. The following day he died. Just after, my informant Joseph was sitting in his armchair, when he felt a sharp tug at his sleeve. This he regarded as a sign from his brother that he had safely made the trip into the spirit world. These events occurred in 1965, but Joseph believes he experienced astral projection when he was three or four years old. At the time he slept in the same bedroom as his parents and recalls vividly the night when he seemed to be floating above their bed and looking down at them.

The Cacchionne family are by no means unique in Staffordshire and the tales to be told are many and varied. All could be ascribed to mundane causes, though the people who have these experiences are in no doubt about the nature of the apparitions. Here is a quotation from Joseph Cacchionne's original letter to me, in response to a public appeal for information:

. . . I know little about Ghost Stories as you put it, but to me they are no stories but the real stuff . . . there are more things in Heaven and on Earth that the majority of persons don't know about, being too Earthly-minded.

2 Legendary Tales

THE MOST ancient of Staffordshire's legendary tales relates to the Christian Martyrs of Lichfield. Plot, in his *Natural History of Staffordshire,* has this to say:

> Nor have I more to add of *British antiquities* but that a ground called *Christianfield* near *Stitchbrook* in this *County,* is said to be the place where St *Amphibalus* taught the *British Christians* converted by the Martyrdom of St *Alban,* who flying from the bloody persecution of *Maximian* raised in *Britan An.* 286, followed him hither 84 miles, as *Ross* affirms it, from the place of their conversion; where the *Romans* that were sent after them [...] finding them in the exercise of their Religion, tooke them and carryed them to the place where *Lichfield* now is, and martyred 1000 of them there, leaving their bodies unburyed to be devowered by *birds* and *beasts,* whence the place yet retains the name of *Lichfield* or *Cadaverum campus,* the field of dead bodies to this very day, the *City* bearing for their *Device,* rather than *Armes,* and *Escocheon* of *Landskip* with many *Martyrs* in it, in severall manners massacred:

Another version of the story is that the one thousand Christian Anglo-Saxons were an army who fought a battle with the Romans. The attack on the Emperor Diocletian was led by three chieftains, who were slain alongside their men. They are recalled in a single verse of doggerel:

Three slain Kings named Borrow, Cope and Hill,
When the battle was ended, lay quite cold and still.
Legs, arms and bodies were scattered all about,
For the battle had been cruel, of that there was no doubt.

The field on which the Christians were killed was to become the site of Lichfield cathedral.

Two further ancient legends are concerned with the martyrdom of Christians. The first, from Stone, is the tale of Wulfad, eldest son of Wulfere. His royal father had taken the Catholic faith in name only, in order to marry Erminilda who, through her mother, carried the family line of the Saxon Kings and the blood of the saints. Wulfad, like the other children, was influenced by his mother's gentle and caring ways and, well before he had heard the term Christian, he began to live his life like one. One day, while out hunting, Wulfad and his hound became separated from the main hunt in pursuit of a doe. The hound eventually lost the scent completely and Wulfad, unsure of his way in virgin woodland, decided to follow a stream in the belief that it would lead him out of the wood. The stream eventually brought him to a thickly wooded glade in which he discovered a cave. He heard the sound of a voice in prayer coming from the cave and, on entering, found a hermit in prayer in front of a crude alter and crucifix. The hermit, St Chad, spoke with the boy and, by the time he left the cave, he had decided to become a Christian and later brought his brother, Rufin, to visit the holy man. On one of these visits the boys were tracked to the cave by Werbode, a close friend and favourite of the king. Werbode reported that the boys were being taught to rebel and, on the next visit, the king accompanied him and, again, they listened at the cave entrance. This time the boys were receiving Holy Communion and, when they refused to renounce their new faith, Werbode murdered both of them. Later, the king repented of his part in the death of his sons and adopted the faith under the guidance of St Chad.

The final tale of Christian martyrdom describes the murder of St Kenelm. In 819, following his father's death, Kenelm became King of the Mercians at the age of seven. The young monarch was left in the care of his father's sister, who soon handed him over to an officer called Askbert, with instructions to do away with the boy; Quenedrida or Quendred, the sister, had designs upon the throne. Plot then takes up the story:

... he had the young King into *Clent wood* in this *Country*, under the fair pretense of taking pleasure in hunting, and when he had gotten him into a suitable place, he cut off his head, and buryed him where no man knew but himself, till discovered by a certain *Cow* of widdow woman, that would feed no where but beside *St. Kenelms* grave; and a *Scrole* dropt by a white *Dove* upon the altar of *St. Peter* at Rome, as Pope *Leo minor* or *Leo* the *third* was celebrating *Mass,* containing these words:
In Clent kau bathe kenelin kinebearn lieth under thorn headed
   by reabed:
which none of the *Romans* understanding, it was shewed to the people of the several *nations,* amongst which a *English-man* there present, rendered it into *Latin,* ... Englished thus
   In Clent *in Cow-bach under a Thorn*
   Lyes King Kenelm *his head off shorne.*
..., order was presently sent by the pope to *Wolfred* the Arch-Bishop of *Canterbury,* and the rest of the English *Bishops* to search and take up his *body,* which was accordingly done and carried in great state to the *Abby* of *Winchelcomb Glocestershire* of his *Fathers* foundation, and there honorably buryed.

Plot noted that the name Cowbach or Cowdale, as it was also known, was still in use in the late seventeenth century and the area lay about half a mile to the north-east of Clent church; the local legend was quite clear in attributing the name to the attendance of the cow on the unmarked grave of Kenelm.

An interesting tale revolves round Sir John Chillington, sixteenth-century owner of Chillington Park, near Wolverhampton. Sir John was a famous sportsman, but his interest in animals also led him to make one of the first zoological collections this country has known. The animals were kept in cages on different parts of the estate, and were tended by a specially chosen and well-trained team of keepers. In spite of all precautions, a panther, Sir John's favourite beast, escaped and he and his son went in pursuit. They came upon it about a mile from the main house; it was crouched behind a bush, ready to pounce on an unsuspecting mother and child. Notwithstanding the great range and his breathless state, Sir John raised his cross-bow. His son, fearing he might miss, called out:

> *Prenez haleine; tirĕz fort.*
> Breathe deep; pull hard.

The words caused the knight to pause and steady himself. The panther sprang, but the bolt flew home, and the animal fell dead a yard in front of the child. A cross was erected on the spot, thereafter known as Giffard's Cross, and Sir John took his son's words as a new family motto. An old, worn and heavily weathered cross still stands in the garden of the lodge, about a mile from Chillington Park Hall, on the road from Codsall to Brewood; it is said to be the original Giffard's Cross, erected in 1651.

In more recent times, the origin of some legendary tales is disputed. The Bishop's Stones at Weeford were said to be placed at the roadside in memory of a Bishop of Lichfield who, along with his attendants, was killed by robbers as they travelled the road; the stones were piled at the spot where each dead body was found. A more mundane account is that the stones were placed in piles on the instructions of John Vessy, Bishop of Exeter, in the reign of King Henry VIII. During a visit to the area, the Bishop had been obliged to travel the road while transacting his business and, finding the loose stone dangerous to his horse and those of other travellers, he commissioned the poor of the parish to gather them up and place them in piles.

Staffordshire also has a version of the tale of the Wandering Jew. The original story relates how Jesus, upon leaving Pilate's tribunal, stopped on the steps of the Hall of Justice to ask a Jew for water. The man refused, saying to Jesus, 'Walk on Jesus, go quickly, why do you tarry?' Jesus replied, 'I walk on, but thou shalt tarry till I return.' Since that day the Jew has wandered throughout the world awaiting Christ's return. This Jew is said to be the person who came to the Staffordshire moorlands around Ipstones in the 1650s. It was here that he visited a lame old man, who lived alone in an isolated spot. He knocked at the door one Sunday afternoon and asked for a cup of beer. The old man asked him to take a pot and draw it himself, because his lameness prevented him from doing so. Having taken his drink, the stranger asked him how long he had been ill. The old man told him and the stranger said, 'I can cure you. Take two or three balm leaves steeped in your beer, for a fortnight or three weeks, and you will be restored to your health, but constantly and zealously serve God.' The old man followed these instructions and was very soon healthy again. This Staffordshire story is said to come from Doctor Gilbert Sheldon, later to become Archbishop of Canterbury, who was visiting in the moorlands at the time. A similar tale is told of a stranger, wearing the same purple shag gown, curing another old man in Stamford, Lincolnshire, in 1658.

From Cannock Chase comes the tale of Reynold Radock. During the late eighteenth century he was a young man in his early twenties, studying to be a lawyer in London. He returned home one Christmas with the intention of asking for the hand of his childhood friend and cousin, Bertha Wheatwell. She, unknown to him, had fallen in love with someone else and had no idea that Reynold loved her. He spent Christmas morning at church with Bertha and her parents, and then spent the day at her home. He left late at night still not having put the question and, on his way home, he slipped in the deep snow and was knocked unconscious. He lay outside for some time; eventually neighbours found him and carried him home to bed, thinking that he had merely drunk too much. In the morning the neighbours visited him and found him in serious pain, whereupon they called the doctor. He arrived and diagnosed a critical injury to the spinal column that might, with time, right itself.

In spite of the lavish attentions of an aunt, to whose house he was taken, Reynold did not recover from his injury. He was glad that he had never spoken of his love to his cousin, and their relationship became one of brotherly love. The condition of his body bore heavily on his mind and, after reading and re-reading Defoe's *Robinson Crusoe*, Reynold began to see himself as a moral Crusoe: he resolved to remove himself from the company of the world and live as a hermit on nearby Cannock Chase. He set up home on the Chase and received many visitors, who wished to see and talk with the Hermit of Cannock Chase, as he became known. During his illness he had begun studying the Bible and many came to hear him talk of biblical lore.

After a time his visitors became fewer and he was happy to spend the time in meditation and peace. His only constant companion was a wild hare that had discovered his cell, seeking safety and shelter with him from pursuit by the hunt. Gradually he tamed it and they lived in peace and solitude for a number of years, the creature taking the place in his affections of his lost love, Bertha. One day, within ear-shot of his cell, the hare was taken by dogs and killed; the hermit found her dead body later in the day. Heart-broken at this loss, his grieving made him think of Bertha: the last he had heard was that she had fled from home to marry her lover. Shortly after the death of his hare, he discovered from an old neighbour, who had tended Bertha, the truth of her story. When she had arrived in London, her lover spurned her. By then she was pregnant and decided to return to her parents. On arrival, she found their cottage occupied by others, and learned that her parents had died of heartbreak at the loss of their daughter. At this news she collapsed, physically and mentally exhausted. She was carried to Cannock workhouse and then to the churchyard, where she was buried by the side of her parents. This story broke Reynold's heart as well and, because of his new-found grief and unsociable nature, he lost the last of his visitors and hence the help he needed to feed and clothe himself. In time, broken in mind and body, he was removed to Cannock workhouse, where he died, happy in the knowledge that his last resting-place would be next to his cousin and would-be sweetheart, Bertha. For many years the only memory of the Hermit of Cannock Chase was a stone marking the grave of his pet hare and inscribed with a verse, which ended:

> Each day she did around my humble cot attend;
> She was my sole companion and my silent friend.

In the end, the verse weathered away completely and the stone was lost in undergrowth, so that today there is no reminder of his existence.

The final story is one still popularly told in the district of Tettenhall. It concerns an old gypsy woman who, one Sunday, sat in the base of a tree in the church-yard at Tettenhall, knitting or weaving. The horrified vicar asked her to stop her sacrilegious activity, but she made a blasphemous reply and cursed the church. Soon after she was struck by lightning and buried in the churchyard. Every year it is said that the gravestone moves an inch nearer the old willow tree where she used to sit; the stone itself is etched with a head and torso.

3 The Devil, Witches, Dragons, Giants and Fairies

IT WAS widely believed that the Devil stepped on the blackberries on Michaelmas Day; this is why they should not be picked after that date. He left his mark in local rhymes as well, and a verse once popular in the region of Brewood ran thus:

> At Kyddemoor Green the Devil was seen,
> At Brewood he was shoed,
> At Gifford's Cross he mounted his horse,
> At the Ball of Coven he was put in the oven,
> At Chillington Hall they ate him, bones and all!

Further north he appears in a rhyme that reflects the poor state of the roads in Staffordshire. Muxon is an abbreviation for Mucklestone:

> Audley, Madeley, Keele and Castle,
> Hixon, Muxon, Woore and Aston,
> Ranscliff is rugged, and Wrinehill is rough,
> But Betley's the place where the Devil broke through.

The Black Country of the eighteenth century also gave rise to rhymes illustrating the industrial nature of the area, as well as the Devil's amazement at finding a place worse than his native Hell:

> When Satan stood on Brierley Hill
> And far around him gazed,
> He said, "I never more shall feel
> At Hell's fierce flames amazed."

Having discovered this Hell upon earth:

> He staggered on to Dudley Woodside
> And there he laid him down and died.

Another runs:

> The Devil stood on Bradley Moor
> And heard the forges roar;
> Quoth he, 'I've heard a row in Hell,
> But none like this before.'

He crops up again in a curious Black Country rhyme, said to refer to the harsh, foul language of the nailers:

> The Devil ran through Sedgley,
> Booted and spurred,
> With a scythe at his back
> As long as a swerd [sword].

Finally, from the Staffordshire moorlands, we are assured that it was at:

> Stanton on the stones,
> Where the Devil broke his bones.

There are one or two humorous tales, where folk were fooled into believing that they were visited by the Devil or devils. Dr Robert Plot mentions the circular bare patches in meadow and grassy woodland areas, where devils and witches danced:

... whence some men perhaps may think it probable enough, that some few of these *Circles* (especially the bare ones that have little grass) may sometimes indeed be made by the forementioned mixt dances of *Devils* and *Witches*, . . .

Otherwise there are no further accounts of his activities and appearances in Staffordshire; one or two writers refer to men selling their souls to the Devil but do not give specific tales.

The activities and appearances of witches were much more numerous and we will see how these creatures and other evil spirits might be kept away from person or community in the Turning Year chapter; fern seeds, straw, bells, mistletoe, elder trees and chalk-lines could all be used to ward off malevolent beings at the appropriate time and in the prescribed manner. In South Staffordshire it was commonly believed that all the witches on earth gathered in the moon for 'The Witches Parliament' on Midsummer Night, where they arranged the fate of ordinary mortals for the next year. Not only could witches fly to the moon, it was said; they could also draw the moon down to earth. If the moon showed blood-red through autumnal mists, it was a sign that spirits of the air were abroad, and epidemics would soon follow.

At Midsummer it was customary in many places to send 'sun wheels' flying down the steep hills, burning as they went. On their way home, the villagers carried burning torches to ward off witches and spectres: they would sit at their doors until the brands had burned out. Those who wished to discover a witch applied the following rules, according to Lawley in his *Staffordshire Customs*:

1 If a person was very sleepy in the day time it was a sure sign he or she had been revelling with the devil in the night.
2 To talk with oneself was a sign that the person was talking to his familiar imp.
3 To be seen lurking near the house of a sick person was a suspicious sign.
4 To show sympathy with a witch a sure sign of complicity.
5 To be frightened when accused a sure sign of guilt.
6 To be cool under the same circumstances a sign that the devil was aiding his follower.

Stories of witches and suspected witches are legion. In the early nineteenth century a witch was said to live at Gettliffe's yard in

Derby Street, Leek. Two old women lived in the yard on very friendly terms. The one made a legitimate living baking and selling oatcakes; the other practised as a fortune-teller and a black and white witch. The witch owned a black cat that was mistrusted by the people who lived in the yard: they thought it was inhabited by an evil spirit. The woman who baked oatcakes noticed that, whenever the cat was present, her baking went wrong. One day when the cat was there, and the woman's temper had been tried too far, she threw a partially baked hot cake at the creature. The scalded animal ran crying into the witch's house and the woman followed, determined to tell her friend what she thought of her pet and its tricks. Once inside, the cat was nowhere to be seen, but the old woman had a bad burn on her back and was crying out with the pain.

The idea that witches can turn themselves into other creatures is quite common. Such a woman lived in Hell Lane, Sedgley – re-named Ettingshall Lane by the 1900s – and it was well-known that she could turn herself into a white rabbit and pry about the houses of her neighbours. Witches could also 'fix' their victims, so that they were unable to move. At Cranberry, near Cotes Heath in North Staffordshire, lived an old woman called Hatton who was thought to be a witch. One of her victims claimed to have been fixed on a stile for an hour, and the farm servants, who worked for a Mr Alsop, said they could never transact satisfactory business if they met her on the way to the market.

An interesting trial for witchcraft took place at Burton upon Trent in the reign of Henry VII, 1491, when Richard Bate, a surgeon, was accused by his mother-in-law of making a waxen effigy of her. The common practice was to keep such an image in a warm place and, as it melted, so the life of the person it resembled would waste away also. The surgeon claimed the wax figure was for use as a specific in a case of flux or dysentery, for a woman patient: it did not resemble his mother-in-law, but looked more like 'a jolly water mawkin'. Nothing seems to have been proved against him. Another, and perhaps more common method, was used by a Black Country witch, who would stick a bullock's heart with pins in order to pierce the heart of some person with whom she had quarrelled; sticking objects and effigies with pins seems to have been a universal means of killing through black magic.

Other accusations of witchcraft have occurred more recently. In

1857 a Bromley Hurst farmer, Thomas Charlesworth, found his milk yield dropping; the cheese would not come, the dairy-maid fell ill, and other problems developed in the dairy. One of his labourers suggested that witchcraft was to blame and he should contact one James Tunnicliff, who could put an end to these events. Charlesworth hired Tunnicliff as an exorcist. After some time and several payments, Charlesworth became suspicious of the exorcist and brought a prosecution against him at Stafford for obtaining money by false pretences. Tunnicliff was found guilty and given a year's hard labour for his part in the deception. More typical was an attempt that took place in 1884 in the Black Country: an old woman, jealous of her neighbour's business success, was believed to have put a spell upon her rival. She had been seen visiting the chemist, where she purchased some white powder, which she had placed in a shovel and held over the fire. As the fumes rose, she was heard to mutter a secret incantation. A local reporter visited the old 'witch' and, finding her out, called on the bewitched woman. Apart from stories of other witches long dead, including the discovery by her deceased husband of a bottle containing some brackish liquid, which was buried in the foundations of her house, she was unable to furnish any evidence of witchcraft, and the matter was dropped. The couple took the bottle to a wise woman, who declared it to be a strong spell, but intended for someone else; wise women and wise men played a considerable part in supernatural activities, as we shall see later in the chapter.

Another common trick of witches was transforming articles into something else. A story from Cheadle relates how a woman who was fetching a bag of flour from the local mill passed the time of day with an old witch, who asked her what she had in her bag. She replied, some flour for baking. The witch said it was not flour but manure and went on her way. Although the woman thought this absurd, she could not resist looking into the bag and found that her flour had indeed become manure. She carried it home and left it by the pigsty. Her husband asked why the flour had been left by the pigsty and was told the reason. He told her she was wrong, because flour was spilling out of the bag. They went to look and found that the manure had been turned back to flour. Local people claimed that this was the only time the witch had been known to change something back to its original form.

Various means of protecting oneself against witches have been mentioned elsewhere: we might add the wearing of witch brooches. At one time this was a popular Staffordshire method of counteracting any intended evil spell from an unknown witch. The brooches were of a special design and believed to possess occult powers. St John's wort also offered protection, though, as the following rhyme illustrates, it had to be gathered in a certain manner:

> St John's wort doth charm all the witches away,
> If gathered at midnight on the saint's holy day,
> And devils and witches have no power to harm
> Those that do gather the plant for a charm;
> Rub the lintels and post with that red juicy flower,
> No thunder nor tempest will then have the power
> To hurt or to hinder your houses; and bind
> Round your neck a charm of a similar kind.

A sure means of breaking a spell was to draw blood from the witch. Those who believed a sick person's condition was the result of witchcraft would provide some hard, sharp object to throw at the witch in case she paid a visit in animal form. Blood drawn in this way would break the hold; so would blood drawn from the witch in human form. This cure was used to thwart a Bilston witch. The events took place in the early 1800s in Walsall Street, Bilston. An old woman who lived with her daughter was offended by a neighbour from whom she wished to borrow some household item. The old woman was thought to be a witch and, when the neighbour began to feel various pains in different parts of her body, she and her friends were convinced that the old woman had caused them by her spells. Various remedies were tried, without success, which seemed to confirm their opinion. The following day the neighbours learned that the bewitched woman had been visited at midnight by a huge black cat which sat on her bed, hissing and spitting at her. She was advised by one of her neighbours, who had lived next door to a witch-finder some years before, that she should keep a sharp knife by her side and 'when the demon appeared again, to throw it with all her force, assuring her that if she could wound it so as to draw blood, the witch's power over her would instantly cease'.

That night she was visited again by the cat, and threw the knife with all her force, catching it on the face and drawing blood. The animal fled up the chimney and disappeared. The next day the patient had lost all her pains and felt quite well again. Later the old woman, who was thought to be a witch, was seen to have a cut on her face. Her daughter protested that she had struck her mother and drawn blood, during the course of an argument; as the two were always arguing, this seemed quite plausible. But there were some who stuck to their opinion and the village began a witch hunt, ending with a visit by the policeman and a mob of people at the woman's home. Mother and daughter were out when the group made their call but the policeman searched the house and produced somewhat inconclusive evidence of witchcraft: an old almanac with astronomical signs, a dried snake-skin, a three-legged pot, and a three-legged chair. These were insufficient to convince the policeman, but the almanac and snake-skin were enough to turn the episode into a legend as far as the villagers were concerned.

A less-popular method of warding off evil spells, practised in the eighteenth century, was to obtain the thigh-bones from a body in the churchyard and place them crossways at the foot of the bed each night. An alternative was to wear a piece of rope which had hanged a murderer. An old Bradley man confided to G. T. Lawley, the local folklorist, that he always wore a strand of the rope that hanged Abel Hill at Stafford in 1820, to prevent witchcraft. It was important not to let unbroken egg-shells get into the hands of a witch, as this could be fatal – an idea particularly related to Easter eggs.

Wise men and wise women, sometimes known as white witches, since their sorcery produced good rather than evil, were common in the County and stories of their activities are numerous. One of their main concerns was locating lost or stolen property and, as late as 1891, a butcher at Fox (Ipstones) visited a wise woman at Leek, to recover some stolen meat. The woman gave him a crystal in which he saw the thief. A famous north-County wise man was 'Oud Elijer Cotton', who lived between Fenton and Longton. He was consulted by many Stone people: one client arrived and found some half a dozen people waiting to see him. Further south, in Wolverhampton, the churchwardens consulted a wise man when the church was robbed in 1529 and, at about the same time, the Bilston church-wardens also enlisted the help of a wise man for the same purpose.

A famous Black Country wise man visited by many south Staffordshire folk was Devil Dunn from Dudley. Dunn, who died in

1851, attracted clients from as far afield as London and Scotland, though most of them were local. He claimed to be able to locate stolen property by using charms and many of his clients were wealthy, well-educated people. Nearby at Sedgley lived another wise man, known as Modges, who also earned part of his living by locating stolen goods. An interesting tale is told of a Hell Lane wise man, Old Nicholls, who was consulted by the miners of one particular pit because the candles kept disappearing: though all who worked the pit had been searched, the candles still disappeared mysteriously. Old Nicholls told them that the Devil was stealing the candles. They should go down the pit, one of them carrying a Bible, and, when they heard anything coming, they should read the Lord's Prayer backwards. This, he assured them, would rid them of the Devil permanently. The next night they went to the pit and settled down with Bible and matches all ready if the Devil came. After a long and weary vigil they heard a strange scratching sound. The Bible-reader started up, and matches were struck to give light. What did they see but a large number of rats eating the candles, though they scampered quickly away when the matches were struck. The standing and credibility of Old Nicholls suffered for sometime after this error of judgement.

White witches are less common today, but Staffordshire does have its covens. Recently the *Express and Star,* a Wolverhampton-based daily evening newspaper, reported that two members of a Walsall coven had opened a shop in Freer Street, Walsall, to sell the equipment used by white witches. The shop sells potions, books and other goods. The Walsall coven of six witches recently staged a two-hour ritual, in an effort to help a climber recover from injuries sustained in a bad fall.

Lawley, in his *Staffordshire Customs*, describes a common method of divining to find the whereabouts of stolen property:

> . . . they took the front door key of the dwelling in which the robbery had been committed and placing it carefully on the 18th verse of the 50th Psalm, tied it there. Two persons then held it by the bow of the key on the first finger of their right hands. The names of the suspected persons and the verse from the Psalm were repeated. If the Bible moved at any particular name, that person was considered guilty.

Dragons seem to have made little impression on the folk-memory of the County and the only item that has come to light is a brief rhyme about Wednesbury that Hackwood gives in his *Olden Wednesbury*:

> The Dragon of Wednesbury churches ate –
> (He used to come on Sunday) –
> Whole congregations were to him
> A dish of Salmagundi.
> The corporation worshipful
> He valued not an ace
> But swallowed the Mayor, asleep in his chair,
> And picked his teeth with the Mace.

Giants are seldom mentioned either in Staffordshire folklore, though it is recorded that in Offley Hay there is a sycamore tree, said to have grown from a stake driven through the body of a giant to keep him down. The only other reference to giants seems to be the legend of Holy Austin Rock. The story goes that a giant lived there with his very beautiful wife. Close by, at Enville, was another giant whose rock fortress was known as Samson's Cave. During the course of a drought the giant of Holy Austin Rock was obliged to fetch water from a stream that trickled round the shoulder of Kinver Edge: the drops collected in a stone trough still known as the Giant's Water Trough in the early twentieth century. One day, while he was getting his water, the Enville giant called on his wife, leaned through the top window, and kissed her. The husband returned early and found them. The Enville giant ran off. His enraged neighbour picked up a long stone, shaped like a javelin, and hurled it after him. The stone fell on its end, embedded in the ground, and was ever after known as the Bolt Stone. It was not standing when Hackwood heard the story in the 1900s and, at about that date, the trough was broken up and the giant's spring diverted.

Fairies appealed to local imagination far more than their giant counterparts though fairy lore is not extensive in Staffordshire; the story of fairies who continually moved the foundation stones of the church on a site between Bilston and Wednesfield is told in the December section of the Turning Year chapter. The churches at Walsall and Hanchurch were removed from their original sites by

fairies. Walsall church was 'being built at Churchery, one of the
suburbs of the town; that situation not being pleasing to them, they
removed the foundations to the hill, where St Matthew's now stands.
The vicinity is, according to popular belief, peopled by the little folk
who still gambol there'; so C. H. Poole tells us in his *Customs,
Superstitions and Legends of the County of Stafford.*

Will o' the Wisp or Jack o' the Lantern, the Puck-like character
who led men astray in mines and on moorland, is likewise mentioned
in the Ghosts and Graves chapter. Puck was a well-known fairy in
Staffordshire and his role seems to have been two-fold. In *Staffordshire
Folklore* Lawley tells us of the Puck who 'was said to mislead and vex
people as they journeyed by assuming various shapes, now as a log
in the path over which they stumbled, or as a mastiff who snapped
at their calves, or as a feeble old man who, if the traveller helped him
on, would, when the man was weary, turn into a child and run away
laughing'. These were sometimes mean tricks. He could be sullen
and spiteful, his tricks becoming more frightening – for instance
assuming hideous shapes in order to terrify people. However in
Staffordshire tradition he was never a malevolent Will o' the Wisp,
even though some of his activities resembled them. Another fairy
known in Staffordshire was Lob Lie By the Fire, an awkward,
unprepossessing dwarf, who spent much of his time lurking in the
chimney-corner. He was thankful for the food with which a
household might provide him and, during the night, he fetched
wood and water and carried out other practical jobs. If he took
offence, he could also be peevish, causing soot to fall into the stew,
pulling the bed-cloths from sleeping humans, putting out the fire,
upsetting the spinning-wheel, and making the bread heavy. Then he
would desert the household, never to re-appear.

Of these mischievous fairies the least unkind is Robin Goodfellow
who, as his name implies, is 'a merry imp who plays pranks on
simple people for sport, never for injury'. He would join in children's
games, play bo-peep with travellers, tumble travellers down on the
grass, assume the likeness of a log near the fire-place, then jump up
and dance round the room, and gambol for a bowl of milk. His
character was that of the village wit, without the least animosity or
malevolence towards his human friends. Those who used bad language he disliked and avoided Unlike Lob Lie By the Fire he was a
happy-go-lucky fairy, who did not perform any household tasks.

Another group of fairies are the traditional little people, beautiful in their physical appearance, and helpful and thoughtful in their everyday lives. They inhabit the woods, glens and glades, combat evil, do good and generally lead blameless lives; they were as well-liked in the Staffordshire woods and fields as they were in Irish pastures or on Scottish hillsides, and they were particularly well-loved by the children of the County. They were not infrequently seen by late travellers singing and dancing in their magic circles beneath a full moon. Dr Robert Plot devotes several pages to fairy rings in his *Natural History of Staffordshire*, where he describes them in detail:

> And here perchance by the way it may be no great digression, to enquire into the nature and efficient cause of those *Rings* we find in the *grass*, which they commonly call *Fairy circles*: Whether they are caused by *Lightening*? or are indeed the *Rendezvouses* of *Witches*, or the dancing places of those littel *pygmy Spirits* they call Elves or Fairys? . . . for I have always observed that that the *Rims* of these *Circles*, from the least to the biggest, are seldom narrower than a *foot*, or much broader than a *yard*; some as bare as a path way in many parts of them, others of a *russet* tinged colour (both of these have a *greener* grass in the middle) and a third sort of a *dark fresh green*, the *grass* within being of a *browner* colour; the first kind seldom less than five or six yards *Diameter*, and the other two of various *Magnitudes*; And all these again, as well imperfect, as perfect; some of them *Quadrants*, and others not above *Sextants* of their respective *Circles*.

Plot eventually put the cause of the circles down to the activities of animals, the striking of lightning and the constituency of the soil, though his educated and sceptical approach was certainly not shared by the ordinary folk, who went on believing in them as Fairy Rings.

The good fairies often subjected humans to a test before rewarding them and their gifts were often withdrawn if the person spoke of the reason for his good furtune. A tale said to date from the time when the Black Country was still open farm-land embodies these ideas. A very poor but kind-hearted old lady was returning one day to her humble cottage, which stood a little further down the lane under an elm tree. Suddenly she stopped, for she heard a faint cry coming from the hedgerow. She went to look and discovered a beautiful little child, no bigger than her arm, sitting under a thorn bush, weeping loudly. Her heart went out to the little one, for she had given birth to several children, but they had all died, so she took the infant in her arms and carried it home. Once indoors, she kindled the fire, prepared some warm milk, and watched the child feed. Its bright, intelligent face seemed to her too refined for an ordinary baby, and the idea grew in her mind that she had a fairy infant in her care. Eventually she settled the baby by singing it an old nursery song, and fell asleep herself. When she woke the child had gone, but lying on a little round table in the room was a golden coin. With this the old woman was able to buy all her necessities and, when it was spent, she found another coin. This continued, with occasional visits from the fairy child, whom she fed and sheltered, the child always leaving before morning. Although the neighbours were curious about her new-found independence, she kept her secret until, in an unguarded moment, she confessed what had taken place to a local gossip. As soon as she had spoken, she regretted it, but to no avail, for the fairy never returned.

Sometimes the fairies took a human child, leaving one of their own kind in its place. The human child was taken to fairyland, where it had to remain until it was seven years old. For this reason it was once thought necessary for mothers to keep a close watch on their children until they were christened; after christening, the fairies had no power to abduct a child. G. T. Lawley suggests that many of the very early Staffordshire christenings, which took place when the babies were two or three days old, occurred because of this belief. It was also thought that mentally deficient and physically weak children would, after seven years, be taken to fairyland and the real child restored; they were known as 'changelings'. There is a tale once told at Ipstones about the fairies swapping a child. The event occurred at Bradshaw Farm, when a woman who lived at the farm took her young baby to the hayfields, laid it on a pile of hay protected from the sun and then went to help the haymakers. When she returned, she found her own child had been removed and a fairy left in its place. She took the child home and cared for it as if it were her own and, although she was disappointed, because the child turned out to be a hopthrust or lower-class fairy, she was happy because, whenever she wished for money, she found sums hidden in different parts of the house. The child, who never learned to talk, died when it was a few years old, and the cash payments stopped immediately.

In the same area it was generally believed that, if bits of cake were left about the house, the fairies would come to eat them and, in return, would carry out various household chores and help to churn the butter. If cake was not put out, they would simply steal some from the pantry by climbing through the key-hole. A tale is also told of a tenant farmer at Lady Meadows, who broke his plough, but was too poor to pay for its repair. However, a few days later, the farmer went to look at the broken plough and found that it had been mended. His wife had always been good to the little people, leaving food for them, and so on, and the couple attributed the miraculous repair to the fairies' gratitude.

The south Staffordshire colliers also had their fairies, whose activities in the mines ranged from helpful tapping, warning of impending disaster, to malevolent behaviour endangering life. In mischievous mood they might steel the candles, hide picks and clothes, make mysterious noises, jump from behind pillars of coal and generally cause a nuisance. These knockers, as they were called, could also befriend a miner and help him in his work. The following story is told of a Darlaston miner, Ben Crowder, who worked the pits before the coming of gas and railways. Unlike the other miners, he scorned stories of devils, imps and bad fairies in the mines. On one occasion the men in his pit heard the mysterious knockings associated with the knockers and danger, so they all quickly left the pit. Ben Crowder stayed on and, when the miners came down the following day, they expected to find him dead or injured but, to their amazement, they found him asleep, beside a huge pile of coal; more than twice as much as any one man could expect to hew in the time. They woke him up and, though he refused to make any comment, he told them to come to the pub that evening. So saying, he got in the skip and went to the surface.

That evening the miners crowded into the Old Bush to hear what Ben had to say and, after the usual round or two of drinks, he started his story:

When yo chaps lef' me all bi miself I own up I was 'nation lonely and above a bit oneasy as to what would happen, but after a bit I set to work and for two or three hours sid nothin'. All at once

I looked round an' was above a bit supprised to see a lot of little figures 'bout as tall as a three 'ear old, drest in funny clo's wi tall red caps on the yeds. They looked so funny that I bust out laughin'; at that they begun to laugh to, such curious laughs that sounded like the tinklin' o tay spoons in cups and saucers. Then I begun to use my pick agen, but that seemed to vex 'em, for they tilted my cap over my eyes, pulled my ears, kicked me wi' their little feet, but did'ner hurt me no more than a fly ticklin'; so I set on to laugh again. Then they begun to play at leap frog over me, an' I had to put down the pick and watch their antics. At last one little chap leapt on my shoulder and turned a summersault back'ards; I clapped my hands and roared again. So he laid hold o' me by mi ears an' swung himself to the roof, and begun to throw lumps of coal at me in which the others joined. This was a bit of a nuisance, but I wudner get out o' temper cos I know'd if I did they would perhaps do me a mischief. Finding I wor to be put out they all vanished, but soon come back, each one carrying a tiny pick, with which they all set to work hewing at the coal, while I looked on sort o' dazed, till the candle went out and I fell asleep, and theer I lay till you chaps woke me up, and theer was the coal they had got, all round me, as proof of what I say.

Ben's description of the knockers and his account of their activities naturally fitted in with the legendary picture of them, and the choice of a known sceptic to authenticate the story must have been the clincher for many of the miners and children, who heard the tale round home-hearth and tap-room table.

A less-lucky miner features in another story concerning the activities of these little people. He broke an unwritten law of the mining fraternities by going down the pit to work a stint on Good Friday, which was thought very unlucky. Next day, when the men descended the pit, they found there had been an explosion and the broken body of the miner was discovered under a pile of debris. Although he was very badly burned he was still alive; he had lost the sight of one eye and his face was hideously scarred. Later, while convalescing, he told his workmates that some ugly dwarfs had appeared, carrying tapers, and set the mine on fire. Here was proof to back up the old belief that a miner should not go down the pit on a Good Friday.

The last mining story is of Dick the Devil who worked the Ettingshall pit in about 1800. He was a stranger to the district, would work only at night and seemed to produce twice as much coal as any other workmen. The other men decided that one of them should spy on him and, one night, a man was lowered quietly into the workings and made his way to the coalface. It was ablaze with a spectral light and Dick sat smoking his pipe, while a band of imps worked steadily away, leaving behind them an ever-growing mound of coal. The miner cried out when he saw this and turned back. He heard the imps in pursuit but managed to reach the cage and screamed a warning to the waiting miners, who rapidly hauled him up. As he reached the top a thunderous sound came from the pit below and livid flames shot up the shaft. The miner told of his experience and next day they descended the pit to find Dick the Devil lying dead, killed by the imps because another mortal had seen them at work.

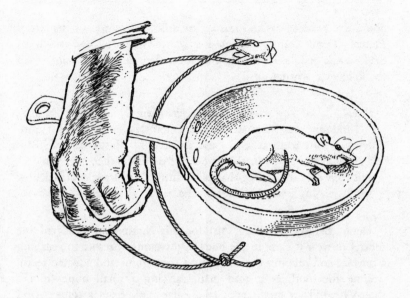

4   Healing Charms and Magic Cures

THE DISPENSERS of healing charms and magic cures were generally ordinary housewives, but the wise men and wise women, whose main activity was the recovery of stolen goods by means of charms, incantations, and other magical techniques, were also consulted about medical matters. In the 1820s an old woman, who lived in the yard of the Hen and Chickens public house, Dudley Street, Wolverhampton, eked out her income by dispensing charms for warts and chin cough, as well as more regular cures for the common ailments; folk medicine includes these ordinary cures, of course, but we are concerned with the specifically supernatural aspects of folk medicine.

Charms were one of the commonest means of curing everyday illnesses and were used in Staffordshire for such widely different conditions as rheumatism and splinters. Toothache was particularly prone to cure by charm if the number of instances where cures have been claimed are anything to go by; perhaps the belief that toothache was a pain straight from the Devil, found on the Staffordshire-

Shropshire border, was the reason for this. The famous wiseman of Dudley, Devil Dunn, dispensed a charm worn by thousands of Staffordshire people. He would give the sufferer a piece of paper with the following written on it:

> Peter . . . sat . . . at the gate of Jerusalem . . . Jesus passed by . . . and said . . . What aileth thee, Peter? . . . Peter said . . . unto Jesus . . . My teeth ache . . . and are sore. . . . Jesus said . . . Rise and walk, Peter . . . in the name . . . of the Father . . . Son . . . and Holy Ghost. . . . He that puts faith . . . in these words I now speak . . . his teeth shall never ache.

Dunn charged a shilling (5p) for this charm and exhorted the sufferer to wear it close to the body. Others might resort to crushing a ladybird and rubbing the remains on their gums and affected teeth, wearing the tooth of a dead man, carrying a small bone from a sheep's head. They might even take a live mole from a trap, cut off its paws before it was dead and wear them. In this case, if the painful tooth was on the right side of the jaw, the left paw was worn and vice-versa.

Whooping cough was also susceptible to charms. One used in the north of the County was the Lord's Prayer, written backwards, sewn up in a piece of linen or silk, and worn round the neck. Whooping cough was a widespread illness and there were other traditional remedies for it. The same woman who used the Lord's Prayer charm gave one of her grandchildren a mouse fried in butter, and claimed that it cured him after the doctors had abandoned the case. The creeping plant known as mouse ear was regarded as an antidote, though no details of how it should be administered are available. A very common method involved taking the child outside to look at the new moon, while the adult rubbed his or her right hand up and down the child's stomach, also looking at the moon, and recting these lines:

> What I see may it increase,
> What I feel may it decrease,
> In the name of the Father, of the Son and of the Holy Ghost,
> Amen.

Another technique was to find a briar on a bramble bush that was growing into the ground at both ends, and pass the child under and over it nine times on three mornings before sunrise, while repeating:

> Under the briar, and over the briar,
> I wish to leave the chin cough here.

This idea of the magical transfer of illness to plants was also tried with reptiles and animals. Cutting the mole's forefeet off and wearing them round the neck was not only a charm, since the illness was believed to transfer itself to the mole: as he died, so the sickness left the child. The toad was treated in a similar manner: its forefeet were severed and hung in a bag round the sufferer's neck. The toad was set free and left to die, taking the chin cough with it. Children were also given rabbits to play with and, after a while, long enough for the chin cough to leave the child and enter the rabbit, the creature was turned loose in the fields; after a short time the child would be free of its ailment. Instead of combining the charm or talisman with the notion of magical transfer, the person might simply wear a protective amulet – a hare's foot, or a hair cut from the cross on a donkey's neck, placed in a silken bag and worn round the neck. The old woman who lived in the yard of the Hen and Chickens public house in Wolverhampton prescribed this donkey-hair cure for babies' chin cough – it was also used for measles; she also placed peppercorn necklaces round the infants' necks and recited 'secret' rhymes over them. As we have seen, transfer of the complaint was also attempted with toothache; the useful mole's foot could effect a cure. The same remedy was used for fits in the north of the County. The tip of the animal's tongue carried in one's pocket would actually prevent toothache.

Warts were the subject of a variety of charms and cures. In 1828 at Stafford the hand of a hanged criminal was used to remove warts and wens; rubbing the affected area with the hand was a common method in the County. There were also wart-charmers who would pass their hands over the affected area a few times and, by the following morning, the warts would have disappeared.

A Miss Devereux, who kept a school for boys at Eccleshall in the mid 1820s, had a particular reputation for charming warts. The story is told of two brothers who were her pupils. They both suffered from the complaint. She gave each of them a small parcel and told them to throw it away, without looking inside. One did as he was told and his warts disappeared; the other looked inside, and found some grains of wheat – his warts remained. Other means of magical transfer were attempted: the wart could be rubbed with a piece of beef – which had to be stolen – and then buried. As the beef decayed, so the wart wasted away. Similarly it could be rubbed with a piece of beef, not necessarily stolen, which was then placed on a thorn. As it dried up, so the wart disappeared. They could also be rubbed with two halves of an onion, which were then buried to obtain the same result. Failing these methods, warts could be blown on when the new moon was first seen, or rubbed at sight of the new moon, reciting meanwhile:

New moon, true moon, take my warts away.

Dipping the afflicted area in the blood of a newly-killed pig was also said to be effective, and a proven method was to rub the warts night and morning with the tail of a tortoise-shell tom-cat during the month of May. Powkes or sties on the eye only appear to have been cured by rubbing a wedding-ring across the affected part nine times on nine successive mornings, while repeating a secret incantation. This method resembled 'rounding', used to draw the hurt from an affected area. Splinters might be removed this way, failing other means. The charmer would slowly draw the middle finger round and round the wound in an ever decreasing circle, completing the sequence by making the sign of the cross over the point where the splinter had entered. Why the middle finger should be used is not specified, but it is the ring finger, and wedding-rings play a part in a number of charms and cures.

Rheumatism might be warded off by carrying a potato in a pocket; this charm could also be used to *cure* rheumatism. Alternatively, the sufferer would be advised to keep a powerful magnet in the pocket. Cramp was dealt with by drawing the stocking on to the left leg first, or by chanting:

The devil is tying a knot in my leg –
Mark, Luke and John I beg
Crosses three now mark to ease us,
For the Father, Holy Ghost, and Jesus.

Mumps were cured by walking blindfold three times round a stream of water, while a bleeding nose was treated by putting a white stone or key down the back, a method still commonly suggested as a cure. Chilblains were said to respond if the patient were held down by two strong boys, while a third thrashed his foot with a handful of prickly holly. Shingles were cured by smearing the affected area with blood drawn from the tip of a black cat's tail. The final charm, the 'eaglestone', a stone taken from an eagle's nest, was widely used for easing labour pains. The old moorland woman who owned a Staffordshire stone, hired it out to women in labour on a time scale.

At Wolverhampton's Collegiate Church it was customary to place mistletoe on the altar during Christmas Eve. Afterwards, it was distributed among the people. They esteemed it, since it was thought that mistletoe blessed on the altar possessed miraculous medicinal powers, particularly in the case of fever. G. T. Lawley records that belief in these healing powers was still popular among the older folk at the turn of the century.

Magical transference was also used to rid miners of choke-damp. A turf was removed from the earth and the sufferer lay face down, with his mouth over the hole; the drawing action of the earth was supposed to drain off the gases. The disease known as the King's Evil, scrofula, was believed to be cured by the touch of a monarch and a number of Staffordshire people obtained certificates. One of them was Dr Johnson, whose mother took him to London to be touched by Queen Anne in 1712, when he was a child of about three.

There were two elaborate transfer cures used for afflicted Staffordshire cattle. The first involved the disease Foule. Writing in his *Natural History of Staffordshire,* Plot says:

[The disease] which sometimes falling into their leggs and feet, causes such impostumes or cores of putrified matter, that they cannot goe farr. . . . They strictly observe the turf where the oxe, cow, or heifer that is thus distempered, sets his sick foot when he first rises in the morning, upon which they usually find some of the sanies or matter of the impostume, press't out by his weight: this very turf, with the impression upon it, they cut up, and hang upon a tree or hedg towards the north wind, which blowing upon it, the beast becomes cured in three or four days.

Plot heard of the use of this cure round the Tamworth area in 1685. He also writes that a shrew mouse, coming into contact with the body of horse, cow or sheep, would cause the animal to lose the use of a limb. Many farmers kept a 'shrew ash' handy. This, when applied to the limb of the beast, cured it of the affliction. A 'shrew ash' was made by boring a hole in the trunk of an ash tree. When the cavity was deep enough, a live shrew mouse was put in the hole and sealed in, while secret incantations were recited. Sometimes several mice were used. The twigs of the tree then possessed magic powers which lasted for ever. This could be done with oak and elm trees, as well as ash; and the tree was then known as a nursrow tree.

Two rather odd variations on the theme of magical transfer complete our survey of charms and cures. The first, a remedy for croup, was not infrequently used by Staffordshire colliers and forgemen, according to F. W. Hackwood, a local historian. They would hold a warm, living pigeon to the throat of the child, and then let the creature die of starvation. As the bird died, so the croup left the child. Pigeon-flying was a very popular sport and such a gesture would be regarded as a great sacrifice by the men. Finally, an item from Wells Bladen's *Folklore of North Staffordshire*, entitled 'Cure by Sympathy':

Mr Leedam, of The Leasows, has given me particulars of an old and very curious custom. Some eight or nine years ago a valuable colt, belonging to him, was accidentally staked. After the farrier had attended to the wound, the old gardener, Robert Fairbanks, of Sharpley Heath, came to his master and begged permission to dress the stake, which had inflicted the injury, with the ointment, declaring that if he did so it would fester as well as the wound, and the latter would quickly heal. He was very indignant when his master refused to sanction the experiment being tried.

5 From the Cradle to the Grave

IN MANY present-day Staffordshire households life is still directed, to some extent, by the do's and don'ts reflected in traditional beliefs and practices handed down from generation to generation; these usually revolve round the important occasions like birth, marriage and death, but sometimes occur in day-to-day living, as in the notion that bad luck follows if new shoes are placed on a table before being worn, or if two people cross on the stairs.

Birth used to be rich in traditional beliefs, but now, except for crossing the baby's palm with silver to bring him wealth in later life, most modern mothers have discarded them. In the late nineteenth century many thought it extremely foolish to go against traditional advice. The modern practice of weighing a baby at birth would have been frowned on by most working-class mothers and grandmothers: weighing at birth was thought very unlucky, and meant the child would die before the year was out. Likewise, to ensure a successful life the baby, when first taken from its mother's arms, would be carried upstairs, not down. Such a child would be sure to 'rise in the world' as an adult. So strong was the belief that some mothers would have the child carried up a specially prepared step-ladder before being taken downstairs. Bad luck was also attracted by cutting a baby's nails or hair before its first birthday, though mother was allowed to bite the nails down; if the palms of the hands were washed, wealth would be washed away.

It was important to keep an eye on the family cat, since it was thought that they 'sucked the breath' of babies with fatal results. After child-birth the new mother would make sure that she was 'churched' before going visiting, and couples who had sufficient children were careful not to rock an empty cradle, since this rocked a new baby into the world. One of the most popular beliefs was that a child born with a caul or membrane covering its face could never drown. Those who possessed a caul were also protected from drowning which meant that the membranes became quite valuable. As a rule they were kept in the family but, when they found their way onto the open market, they fetched a good price. They were sometimes handed down from one generation to the next as the will of Sir John Offley, of Madeley Manor, dated May 1658, illustrates:

> Item, I will and devise one jewell done all in gold enamelled wherein is a caul that covered my face and shoulders when I first came into the world, the use whereof to my loving daughter, ... so long as she shall live: and after her decease the use likewise thereof to her son Offley Jenny during his natural life, and after his decease to my own right heirs for ever, and so from heir to heir to be left so long as it shall please God in his goodness to continue any heir male of my name, desiring the same jewell not to be concealed or sold by any of them.

Unlike the caul, a child's first teeth were burnt immediately, and woe betide Friday's child:

> Never be born on a Friday,
> Choose some other day if you can;
> Or else you will be, like unto me,
> A most unfortunate man.

There seem to be few references to christening in Staffordshire folklore but, if a long dialect poem called 'The Wench they Christened Ben' is to be believed, christening was an unusual occurrence.

The poem describes how Cog Round and his wife, Molly, call the parson to christen their child. They cannot think of a name, so they ask the parson to choose one, and he christens it Ben. After the parson has left, Molly scolds her husband for allowing the child, a girl, to be called Ben and the two argue violently. The anonymous writer comments:

> P'raps at these people's manners you'll laugh
> But surely you'll not be surprised
> When I tell you that was the first
> That was in the city baptised.

Young girls, waiting for their future husbands, satisfied their curiosity with games and charms intended to supply the name of their unknown spouse. At Whitgreave, near Stafford, Charlotte Burne met a housewife who had discovered the name of her future husband with an ash leaf which had its final leaflet missing. Her sister told her to put the leaf above her front door and to note the first male to go in who was not a member of the family: her future husband would bear the same christian name. Sure enough the first arrival was called William and she later married a man of the same name. Similar results could be obtained by various means. At Wednesbury it was customary for a girl to pare an apple, making sure the peel was in a whole, unbroken piece. She would then stand back from her friends and throw the paring over her left shoulder. The nearest manuscript capital letter which the shape of the paring assumed would be the initial of her future husband's name. This custom was usually part of the St Clement bite-apple festivities described in the November section of the Turning Year Chapter. Failing these methods, or for reassurance, a maid could turn to the moon for help:

> When the new moon first showed itself she (the maid) turned her inmost garment on going to bed, saying as she lay on the pillow:

> > New moon, show to me
> > Who my true love shall be.

And she would be sure to see in her sleep the image of her future husband.

Others might visit one of the many old women who could tell them the name of their husband-to-be, or at least supply them with a charm, often a piece of paper, with a name written on it, which would perform the same function. The young men sometimes wore 'bachelor buttons', marsh marigolds, in their pockets and if these did not wither, their courtship would be successful. Jilted girls collected twelve smooth stones and threw them into a pond or pool, calling the name of the faithless lover; by this means he could be brought back. Those who simply wished to recall a lover from a distance bought a pennyworth of dragons' blood, cut a piece of red flannel into a heart shape, and stuck three pins into it – these represented cupid's darts – with the pin-points facing the centre. Dragons' blood was sprinkled on the flannel, which was burnt on the fire as the clock struck midnight. Meanwhile this rhyme was recited:

> 'Tis not this blood I wish to burn,
> But ——'s heart I wish to turn;
> May he neither rest nor sleep,
> Till he returns to me to speak.

This ritual was performed on Friday nights; the last Friday in the month was said to be the best time of all. It was also possible to ensure that the apparition of a lover would appear on the eve of St Thomas's Day, if a sprig of evergreen was placed beneath the pillow at bed-time and the following couplet recited:

> Good St Thomas, stand by my bed,
> And tell me when I shall be wed.

Another means of discovering the date of a wedding was to pluck a hair from your head and thread a finger-ring on it. It was then held over a tumbler, half filled with water, and the number of times it touched the sides indicated the number of years to the wedding. Hair might be used for this purpose, but giving a lover hair, or indeed anything made of hair, was taboo because it cuts love, and the giver will never be married.

We end this brief look at courtship with a short song that was popular in a number of industrial regions, although the words were varied to suit the trades of a particular area. In South Staffordshire the girl comes from a family of nail-makers. It illustrates her attitude to the old custom of marrying into the father's trade, and demonstrates a practical approach to the problem of bettering one's financial position:

> My mother sent me for some water,
> For some water her sent me.
> And in the well I nearly tumbled,
> When my collier lad come whistling me.

> My mother says if I wed a collier,
> It will break her tender heart
> But I don't care what me mother tells me,
> A collier I'll have for my sweetheart.

> For colliers getting gold and silver,
> Nailers getting nothing but brass
> So what wise wench would marry a nailer
> While there's plenty of collier lads.

When courtship was nearly complete and marriage imminent, another set of beliefs, aimed at keeping the couple on the straight and narrow, came into prominence. It was thought very unwise to take a wood-anemone anywhere near a wedding, since it brought bad luck. The belief comes from the north of the County, but more widespread is the theory that a couple should not contemplate marriage on Fridays, or in the month of May, since both were bad times and brought disaster. May, a month dedicated to the Virgin, features in the warning line: 'Marry in May, rue the day' or, in another version, 'Marry in May, you'll soon decay'.

Whereas the fortunate bride would be one on which the sun shone. Hence the old saying: 'Happy is the bride that the sun shines on'.

And a couple who wished to bring themselves luck would be married in:

> Something old and something new
> Something borrowed and something blue

- a rhyme still commonly quoted in the region.

It was a fairly usual belief that bread, which rose excessively and almost toppled over, indicated an approaching wedding, and proverbial sayings such as:

> She who changes her name and not her letter,
> Marries for the worse and not the better

were also widespread and popular during the mid-nineteenth century. The last pre-wedding advice might be that the couple should not sit with their backs to the horses on their wedding day.

In Staffordshire it was customary among the working classes for the bride and bridegroom to go to church unaccompanied either by father or mother, with only the bridesmaids and best man in attendance. However at Bilston it not infrequently happened that the bride was met at the church-door by a party of well-wishers, who would present her with a pair of white gloves. Flowers were and still are an essential part of any wedding and, in the rural parts of Staffordshire, it was once common for the young men to wear 'Bachelors Buttons', no doubt to bring luck to the couple. Further north, at Wolstanton, near Newcastle, the practice of 'playing the bride to church' sometimes took place. This report was printed in the *Wolverhampton Chronicle* on 1 January 1812:

> At the village church of Wolstanton, near Newcastle, on yesterday sen'night Mr Samuel Davies and Mrs Anne Turner were married, both of that place, and whose ages in the aggregate amount to 140 years. . . . The happy bridal party were preceded to church by a band of musicians in token of the high esteem in which they held the bride.

Among the richer families, wedding parties were often escorted by a mounted cavalcade, and, at Stone, wedding parties used the Priory Gate, funerals the West Gate of St Michael's Church, presumably to avoid a meeting which would be thought most unlucky. It is still said that a sweep at a wedding brings good luck.

Once the ceremony was complete, there were a variety of ways in which the occasion was marked by custom. In South Staffordshire most weddings were followed by a sports meeting in which all the villagers would participate, and a popular feature was a game of football. The ball was provided by the bridegroom and known as the 'bride ball'; the game itself was played by large numbers of players in the streets of the villages, rather than on a fixed field with equal numbers to each side. At the home of one Staffordshire family it was customary for the bride and groom to sit astride the handrail of the main staircase, and slide down into the waiting arms of the best man, whose job it was to catch them. The custom was still observed in the early twentieth century, until the house was burned down. At Ipstones and Stanton a different fate awaited the groom as he left the church, for he would find the way barred by a rope, held across the road by the village lads. The groom was expected to hand out some small coins before he could go on his way with the bridal party. The girls present at North Staffordshire weddings generally hoped to be given a piece of wedding-cake, which many of them would place under their pillows at night, so that they might dream of their husbands-to-be.

Specific beliefs relating to the romantic side of married life are few in Staffordshire. It was once widely believed that a married woman should never remove her wedding-ring from her finger, because she would be in danger of losing her chastity if she did and, related to this idea, if a ring should be lost or broken it should be replaced immediately and must be placed on her finger by the husband. On the gloomier side, it was a popular nineteenth-century belief that a seven-year separation 'breaks' the marriage contract. Another accepted means of ending a marriage was wife-selling and there are numerous recorded instances throughout Staffordshire and elsewhere, until well into the nineteenth century; a few odd cases occur at a much later date. The practice had no sanction in law, but it was a matter of general knowledge among the people that, if the prescribed custom was followed, the separation was legal. The general procedure was for the husband to tie a halter round the woman's neck, take her down to the market-gate, where he purchased a toll-ticket, lead her several times round the market, and eventually put her up for auction. If this procedure was followed, in the same way that livestock was sold, they believed it was legal. It is worth noting that, in every documented case of wife-selling in England, the purchaser was previously known by the husband and wife, and the price had been agreed; the sale was merely a legal formality, and public declaration of intent. The *Wolverhampton Chronicle* described one such case that took place in November 1837:

> A strange and unwonted exhibition took place in Walsall Market on Tuesday last. A man named George Hitchinson brought his wife, Elizabeth Hitchinson, from Burntwood, for sale, a distance of eight or nine miles. They came into the market between ten and eleven o'clock in the morning the woman being led by a halter which was fastened round her neck and the middle of her body. In a few minutes after their arrival she was sold to a man of the name of Thomas Snape, a nailer, also from Burntwood. There were not many people in the market at the time. The purchase money was 2s 6d [12½p], and all the parties seemed satisfied with the bargain. The husband was glad to get rid of his frail rib, who, it seems, had been living with Snape three years, erroneously imagining that because he had brought her through a turnpike gate in a halter, and had publicly sold her in the market before witnesses, that he is thereby freed from all responsibility and liability with regard to her future maintenance and support.

However one or two newspapers reported auctions taking place, where a number of men made bids for the wife being sold. *The Staffordshire Advertiser* of 1 March 1800 remarked:

> On Tuesday last – Hodson a chimney sweeper, better known by the appropriate nickname of Cupid, brought his wife into the market place of this town and disposed of her by auction. She was put up at the sum of one penny, but, as there were several bidders, and of course a good deal of rivalship, she sold for five shillings and sixpence. Thus usual delicate ceremony of tying a rope round the woman's neck was dispensed with; . . .

The custom became a popular cause for the regional press, who publicised wife-sales in an attempt to inform the ignorant that the procedure was both illegal and barbaric. In addition it became a subject for comic songs and we have fragments like:

He drove his wife to market
Just as they drive a pig.
With a halter tied round her neck,
Instead of round her leg.
So he put her up by auction,
And he shouted out 'Who'll buy?
Just name a price, my masters,
I don't care what, not I.'

There are also several complete songs on the subject. Many of these
were once popular in Staffordshire and one in particular was probably
composed locally. It described how Bandy Leg Lett set about selling
his wife:

Sally Lett, or a Wife for sale
(A Bilston Ballad)

Ding-a-dong, ding-a-dong,
"O, ha! o, ha! o, ha!"
Ding-a-dong, ding-a-dong!

This is to gi' notice
That Bandy-legged Lett,
Will sell his wife, Sally,
For what he con get.

At twelve o'clock sertin'
The sale'll begin;
So all yer gay fellers
Be there wi' yur tin.

For Sally's good lookin'
An' sound as a bell,
If you'n on'y once heard her
You'n know that quite well.

Her bakes bread quite handy,
An' eats it all up;
Brews beer like a good 'un,
An' drinks ev'ry sup.

Her wears mons breeches,
So all the folk say;
But Lett shouldna let her
Have all her own way.

Her swears like a trooper
And fights like a cock,
And has gin her old feller
Many a hard knock.

So now yo' young fellers
As wantin' a wife,
Come and bid for old Sally,
The plague of Lett's life.

At twelve i' the morning
The sale'll begin;
So yo' as wants splicin'
Be theer wi' yer tin.

Once the sale had been made, it was usual for the three participants, husband, wife and purchaser, to retire to a nearby public-
house to complete the bargain: the husband handing over the
toll-ticket to the new 'owner', the purchaser giving the agreed sum
to the husband. Any required bill of sale was drawn up by a 'clerk'
and the health of the three drunk by the assembled company. Other
common innovations introduced into the proceedings included a
'crying' of the sale by a bellman, the purchase of a brand-new halter
by the seller, and leading the wife through as many as three toll-
gates, in order to make the agreement more binding. It was also
generally accepted that the husband should act as his own auctioneer,
and this is clear from many of the newspaper accounts describing
sales.

It is interesting to add that the right of anyone to sell a woman
was forbidden by the law II Cnut, 74, and that the practice of
marriage brocage was held void by the House of Lords' decision in
the case of Hall *v.* Potter in 1695. Its popularity suffered no set-back
in spite of these two decisions, and the decline of the custom during
the second half of the nineteenth century was due in part to the
introduction of divorce legislation in 1857. Prior to this date, divorce

could only be had through special act of Parliament, a lengthy and expensive procedure.

Those wives who could not reach an amicable settlement with their husbands, and arrange for a selling to take place, might run away from home. At Tutbury such a wife might well have to suffer the indignities of Rough Music and its attendant practices. *The Derby Mercury* reported a case that occurred between 8.00 and 9.00 pm on 5 March 1850:

> Proceedings commenced by a mob assembling in front of the house of the returned fugitive, and demanding that she be given up to its tender mercies. The husband wished the ceremony to be postponed until the morning, but the mob would not be denied, and he then unlocked the door, and delivered her up to the mob, who placed a rope round her waist, and trailed her around the village, blowing cows' horns, ringing bells, shouting, and making other noisy accompaniments. On arriving at a place called the Little Dove, they dragged the woman into the water, and committed all kinds of barbarities; and the night being extremely cold, her state may be better imagined than described. After they had satisfied their feelings, she was then dragged home, her husband having, as we are informed, been a spectator of the whole proceedings.

Recalcitrant wives were not the only recipients of rough justice; those who beat their wives to excess might also find themselves on the receiving end. The custom of laying straw at the door of persistent offenders, to show corporate disapproval of the situation, became common during the late eighteenth and early nineteenth century, and at Marchington the village took the matter much further:

> In Marchington . . . it was the custom of the village fathers to go beyond this symbolism, and mete out personal punishment upon the offender. There it used to be the custom to mount a wife beater astride upon a pole which was carried on the shoulders of the village Dracos. First of all a committee was called, who examined into the matter. If the accused were found guilty, a procession was formed, a cart provided, from which the village

crier or poet, if one existed, recited the culprit's misdeeds, and then the latter was mounted on his wooden steed, and carried round the village, amid the jeers of the people. The poor fellow had as much as he could do to sit safely on his pole, which jolted at every step the carriers took, and his efforts to keep upright caused much amusement.

Lawley wrote this account in the late-nineteenth/early-twentieth century, when such punitive customs had disappeared, though wife-beating was still a common occurrence; the Marchington custom seems to have been at its peak in the late-eighteenth century. It is interesting that a wisp of straw was once used to silence the crowd present at the punishment of a scold; the straw or hayband was held up to the crowd, who were then expected to fall silent. At a later date the same symbol was used on the canals, when it became common practice to place a wisp of straw underneath the arches of the Black Country canal bridges, to indicate that traffic was temporarily suspended, i.e. traffic was absent from the canal, making that stretch of waterway *silent*.

A happier, though seldom successful, custom took place at Wychnor; it was known as the Wychnor Flitch. A flitch of bacon was given to the married couple who could prove that for a full year and one day there had been no domestic dispute between them. It probably dates from 1347 when John of Gaunt, the Lord of Tutbury, instituted it as the means by which Sir Philip Somerville and his successors should retain the manor of Wychnor, which lay within the Honor of Tutbury; this Staffordshire version of the custom is probably earlier than the much-publicised Dunmow Flitch of Essex.

At Wychnor a 'bacon flyke' was hung in the manorial hall throughout the year, except during Lent,

> to be given to everyche mane or womane after the day and the yere of their marriage to be passed; and to be given to everyche mane of religion ... after the yere and day of their profession finished or of their dignity received.

A wooden flitch was hung in the hall until the actual day of the ceremony.

The candidates came to the Bailiff or Porter to apply in person and promised to appear at the appointed time, with two neighbours. On that day the applicant was led in procession to the Hall where he and his neighbours were questioned. Once their testimony had been accepted, the bacon was taken down and laid on a quarter of wheat and a quarter of rye; the claimants knelt down, and swore to the truth of their claim. Finally the Lord of Rudlowe, who held his lands on condition that he executed his duties concerning the bacon flitch, provided a beast to carry away both the meat and the grain. The couple left in procession with minstrels and others in attendance.

There is still a house on the original site of the manor. Wychnor Park, as it is called, stands of the A38 near Wychnor and hanging in its hall is an early wooden replica of the original wooden flitch. Would-be visitors should note that the house is not open to the public.

Apart from specific customs concerning marriage and family life, there were many traditional beliefs and omens current within the County. Many of these still exist and, in a self-conscious way, are partly believed by those who remember them; although they might not be convinced of their accuracy, they observe them 'just in case'. Among the wide variety popular today are the belief that cleaning windows changes the weather. An empty purse should never be given as a present, since it will mean that the receiver will be a pauper all through life, therefore a small coin should be placed inside it. Bad luck is invited if umbrellas are open inside the house, peacock feathers or May blossom are brought indoors, and a broken mirror means seven years' bad luck. Passing on the stairs means that the people concerned will quarrel. Giving knives or scissors as presents is forbidden since they cut friendship, they must always be sold for a penny or so. Care must be taken not to cross knives on the table, look at the new moon through glass, or to stir with a knife, which cuts through the smoothness of life and causes disruptions. These sayings are all current in my own household since my wife, whose parents and grand-parents are Staffordshire folk, insists that the rest of the family observe the traditional customs to avoid bad luck.

Apart from these essentially family and household traditions, there are many others extant relating to more general situations. Thus black cats bring luck if they cross your path, walking under a ladder is unlucky, finding a horseshoe lucky. Spilt salt is ominous, but the omen can be reversed if the salt is thrown over the left shoulder with the right hand. It is also bad luck to thank anyone who picks up a glove. You can make a wish if you see a shooting-star or find a four-leaf clover, although the wish should remain your secret if it is to come true. Like their household counterparts, these general beliefs and others are widely known and frequently quoted.

There are many traditional beliefs based on luck that were popular in the nineteenth century, though seldom encountered in present-day Staffordshire. It was then considered unlucky to start a journey on a Friday, the day of the Crucifixion, and also to turn back, once a journey had begun, or even to say goodbye at a gate and, in certain circumstances, to meet a woman on the way to work. In the north of the County, those who saw a parson in a round hat thought it necessary to touch iron. The Reverend Deacon experienced this in Stoke-on-Trent in the early twentieth century:

> As I walk along, I have been amazed to see the number of girls and younger women – only occasionally older women, and only once have I seen a man do it – . . . who will go out of their way, and even rush across the street, to touch iron, before they actually pass me.

A sighting of magpies can mean a number of things, according to the old rhyme:

> One for sorrow,
> Two for mirth,
> Three for a wedding,
> Four for a birth

whereas to injure or kill a frog is unequivocally unlucky. At Stanton, plucking the Wood Anemone was once thought to bring on thunder-storms, while, at Albrighton, the hawthorn, like the May, is regarded as very unlucky if brought into the house. It was lucky to have a crooked sixpence, while looking at a new moon through the window and turning a chair right round on one leg brought bad luck. It was also unlucky to have a haircut when the moon was waning. The number thirteen was unlucky, and still is, but other odd numbers, like three, five, seven, nine and eleven, can bring good luck. It was believed that if thirteen people sat at a table, the first to rise would die within a year, and Friday the 13th is still regarded as a highly unpropitious day. Misfortune may occur to anyone eating a double nut. A mole on the left arm was considered lucky and at Barlaston this nail-cutting rhyme used to be popular:

Cut them on a Monday, cut them for health;
Cut them on a Tuesday, cut them for wealth;
Cut them on a Wednesday, cut them for news;
Cut them on a Thursday, for a new pair of shoes;
Cut them on a Friday, cut them for sorrow;
Cut them on a Saturday, you'll see your true love tomorrow;
Cut them on a Sunday, cut them for evil,
For all the week long will be with you the Devil.

There was also a fairly extensive body of traditional omens associated with everyday life, though most have now disappeared from our County folklore. The first group of these centre round physical changes and parts of the human body. An itching nose might mean one was going to be 'kissed, cussed, or vexed', while an itchy palm meant money would soon be put in it, particularly if the itchy spot was:

rubbed on wood
It was sure to come good.

Whitish specks on the finger-nails were lucky signs, and their benefit was expressed in the traditional rhyme:

A gift on the thumb is sure to come,
A gift on the finger is sure to linger,

while a white spot on the tongue meant that its owner had been telling lies. A burning sensation in the left ear indicated that someone was speaking ill of you, the same sensation in the right ear meant that someone was singing your praises: this belief is still widely quoted. Hair plays a considerable part in such beliefs and hairy men were said to be born to grow rich. A handful of hair that blazed in the fire meant a long life; a single hair that curled after it had been drawn through the hand was an indication of pride. A once widely held and still-popular belief is that an involuntary shudder means someone is walking over the spot where your grave will be. The very small garden-spider was, and still is, called a money-spider. If someone caught it and threw it over his left shoulder, without looking to see where it landed, he would come into money. The first sighting of a spring lamb would bring luck if its head was turned towards you, bad luck if turned away.

Dreams also had their significance as omens. Three commonly held interpretations were that, to dream of the dead meant you would be plagued by the living, to dream of children brought trouble, and to dream of insects foretold sickness or death. There were also omens expressed through inanimate objects, though few of these are heard today; the horseshoe is one of the exceptions, for to find one is still regarded as lucky. Then, as now, the shoe would be taken home and placed over a door and, if it contained any old nails, this was even better. Knives, as we have seen, play a part in present-day folklore; a further belief maintained that, if a knife fell from the table, a male visitor could be expected, if a fork fell, a female visitor would come. Lighted coals flying from the fire may have very different meanings; round coals for a wedding, long coals for a coffin or death. The soot encrusting the bars of a grate, or hanging in flakes, foretold the arrival of a stranger, if they did not drop into the fire. When this happened, the house-holder clapped his hands near the grate, to create a wind, at the same time reciting the days of the week. The stranger was thought to fly off at the mention of the day he was to come. The breaking of a pudding on its removal from the oven is a sign of rain, while, to the country folk of the County, the early loss of leaves from the trees meant a hard winter; the late loss heralded a good winter.

There are a number of beliefs and omens which can only be realized if the person involved makes actual physical moves to initiate the process. Spitting to encourage good results features in several situations; a tradesman should spit on the first money paid him by a new customer and more profitable dealings between them will follow; when a new moon appears, turn the money in your pocket three times and spit on it for good luck. Anyone who hears the howl of a dog can escape the consequences – death in the family – by removing the left shoe, spitting on the underside, placing the sole upwards on the ground and putting the foot over the place spat upon. This offered protection from harm and stopped the dog howling as well. A run of bad luck at cards might be broken by turning a chair round, while a pin could bring good or bad luck:

> See a pin and let it lie,
> You're sure to want before you die;
> See a pin and pick it up,
> All the day you'll have good luck.

But, conversely:

> Pick up a pin, pick up sorrow;
> Don't pick it up, you'll want one tomorrow.

Giving away a pin was also thought unlucky, presumably because it cuts friendship, as does the giving of knives and scissors. A permanent headache could result if hair combings were thrown outside and carried away by the toads; in some cases toothache followed. The Staffordshire belief that burning ferns brought rain was sufficiently serious for Charles I to write a letter to the Sheriff of Staffordshire requesting that no fern should be burned during his visit. Finally, two beliefs involving birds. Throwing at cuckoos or robins was attended with dreadful consequences, but to capture a wagtail by hand, without using traps or catapults, meant that the boy would marry a lady when he grew up.

In the north of the County various farming operations were affected by custom. Pigs were thought best slaughtered at, or soon after, a new moon to prevent them shrinking and to make them salt well. Seeds sown on Sundays were said not to grow. Hens should be set on a Sunday with an odd number of eggs; before sunset, otherwise all the chickens would be cockerels. The small yolkless eggs laid by hens were thought to bring bad luck if brought in the house. Around Leek the use of charms fashioned in brass, copper, lead or other materials, and engraved with strange letters, were thought to improve yields; they were placed on churns to make the butter come more quickly, on the plough to enable one horse to do the work of two, and on the flail, so that the thresher could work more effectively. They were known as a bee. Family charms to guard against road accidents were also worn on journeys.

The moon has a special place in folklore and, as we have seen, features in a number of beliefs and customs. There are other beliefs connected with it that do not fall into any category, but are quite interesting. Logs that are not felled at full moon will burn dull and dead. If the sun and the moon appear together in the sky, some calamity will take place, and the observer should cross himself three times and bow at the same time. Anyone who slept with the full moon shining on his face would become demented. Finally, an odd moon rhyme from an old inhabitant of Willenhall, who recited it to G. T. Lawley in the late nineteenth century:

> The man in the moon,
> Got up too soon
>   To learn the way of knowledge;
> Seed a man in stocks,
> Who'd burnt his chops,
>   Ateing co'd peas an' porrich
> Said he wi' a grin,
> They'n taken me in,
> I was tode the people wun wise;
> But on my word, they'm quite absurd,
> So he toddled off back to the skies.

Death, like birth, is a time associated with various traditional beliefs and practices. We have already noted omens concerned with howling dogs and dreams of insects, but there were many others. A number were connected with animals and birds. A raven flying over a house meant there would be a death in the family and, if magpies flew over a newly bought cow, the cow was sure to die when the farmer walked it home. A sick cow or horse would not survive if the bran mash was mixed with a pointed instrument; just as giving scissors or knives meant severing friendship, so stirring with a pointed instrument presumably signified cutting the life-line. At one time a wild herd of cattle lived on the Chartley Estate of the Ferrers' family; the birth of a black calf coincided with the downfall of the family and gave rise to the belief that the birth of a spotted, part coloured or black calf meant a death would occur in the family within the year. It was said that this phenomena was observed on various occasions. The belief that a white bird would flutter against the window, just before a death took place, was very widespread in Staffordshire and, similarly, to see a robin perched on a house on Christmas day, meant a death would take place in that family during the coming year; so did a cockerel crowing during the night.

Certain natural occurrences also foretold death. Unusual situations like fruit-trees blossoming, or their fruit ripening out of season, were recognised as forewarnings. So were more normal events: fat guttering from a lighted candle, known as a 'winding sheet', and cinders flying out of the fire. It was unlucky to bring May bloom into the house, as mentioned earlier, but to sweep the house with a May broom meant the head of the household would be swept away too. It was thought that clocks often stopped at the time of a death in a household, and warning knocks, a common omen, marbles rolling downstairs and a diamond-shaped crease folded into a table-napkin all signified death. Occasionally it arose from the flaunting of some taboo, such as carrying a naked light outside the house between Christmas and Candlemas. But the rhyme:

> A clot of blood on the rising moon,
> Foretells a death or late or soon

gave little room for manoeuvre. Very little mention is made of these omens today, though dream warnings are still believed. Train, plane and ship disasters are often claimed to have been the subject of dreams. In some cases the dreamer also claims that they themselves, relatives or friends, would have been involved in the disaster had it not been for the warning in the dream.

In some areas there is a variety of beliefs about ways in which the death agony is prolonged. The only Staffordshire version is the fairly commonly held belief that the dying should not be allowed to lie on a mattress or pillow stuffed with feathers of pigeons or wild fowl. This was known in the north and south of the County.

Once death had claimed the soul, the body was subject to a variety of observances. Coins would be placed on the eyes to keep them closed, a plate of salt left on the body, and personal items and furniture used by the dead person covered with white cloths. To meet a funeral was unlucky, but it is still held that rain means the corpse is happy and the mourners need not grieve overmuch; a ray of sunshine falling on a mourner at the service means he will be the next to die. It was once customary to bury suicides at the dead of night in a corner of the cemetery. One such Staffordshire burial is recorded in *Stafford Gaol and its Associations*, where the author recounts the case of a collier who cut his wife's throat, then his own. A verdict of *felo de se* was returned and the police carried out the burial in the prescribed fashion.

There were also a number of beliefs concerning the corpse – the first is also an omen of death. If the right thumb of the body did not stiffen after death, another death would follow. At Eccleshall in 1876 an old woman was found drowned in her well. The body was removed and laid out on the turf. The area where the corpse had rested became a peculiar green and neighbours pointed to this as evidence that she had died by foul means. The last item is a North Staffordshire belief that those who see a dead body and do not touch it would be followed by bad luck.

One of the classic tales of death and the spirit returning to visit a loved one is told in the song *Cold Blows the Wind*, which was widely sung in the Midlands. Our Staffordshire version comes from George Dunn of Quarry Bank. George was still singing the ballad at the time of his death in 1975 when he was in his late eighties. It tells of the return from the grave to visit a loved one and mentions the ancient belief that excessive grieving disturbs the dead:

Cold Blows the Wind

Oh cold blows the wind over my true love,
Cold blows the drops of rain,
I never, never had but one true love,
And in greenwood he was slain.

But I'll do as much for my true love
As any young lass can do;
I'll sit and I'll weep right o'er his grave
For a twelve month and one day.

When twelve month and one day had passed
This young man he arose
And said, 'What brings you here by my grave side
And I can take no rest?

'Go fetch me a note from the dungeon so deep,
Fetch water from a stone,
Or milk white out of a fair maid's breast,
When a fair maid never had none?'

'Give me a kiss from your clay cold lips,
One kiss is all I crave.
Give me a kiss from your clay cold lips
And return back to your grave.'

'If you have a kiss from my clay cold lips,
My breath's so earthly strong,
If you have a kiss from my clay cold lips,
Your days will not be long.'

6 The Turning Year

January

MANY OF Staffordshire's New Year customs are no longer practised, although a considerable number are still common knowledge. First footing is still observed and this account from an undated late nineteenth-century newspaper article on *Midland New Year Customs* describes current practice equally well:

> ... it is considered unlucky to leave the house on January 1st until the New Year has been "let in", and "A pocketful of money, a cellar-ful of beer, and a good fat pig to last yer all the 'ear" has been sung at the door. Efforts are made to induce a dark-haired male person to enter the house first and to wish the inmates 'a happy New Year', and it is deemed most unfortunate for a woman to be the 'first foot'. Many cases of sickness are said to have resulted when such an incident has happened.

The usual rhyme that accompanied 'first footing' ran:

> The cock sat up in the yew tree,
> The hen came chuckling by;
> I wish you a merry Christmas
> And every day a pie;
> A pie, a pie, a peppercorn,
> A good fat pig as ever was born,
> A pocketful of money,
> A cellar full of beer;
> And a good fat pig to last you all the year.
> And pray God send you
> All in a joyful
> New year, a new year, a new year.
> Pray God send you a joyful
> And a happy New Year.

This and similar rhymes would be sung by the men and boys as they moved from door to door on their first footing rounds. Many of them would have just finished celebrating the death of 'Old Tom', as the old year was known, with a brief mock funeral in his honour. Meanwhile their wives and those who remained at home would open their front doors, just on the stroke of midnight, to let in a gust of air and with it the New Year. Villages and towns would then be filled with the ringing of church bells and the Wassail-bowl was passed round, each person expressing some seasonal sentiment as their turn came to drink. In the industrial regions the pealing of the bells was generally accompanied by the works 'bulls' or sirens and the clashing of hammers on iron plates. The church bells were rung with a muffled peal for some time before midnight but the bandages were removed at the stroke of midnight and a merry peal rang out to welcome the New Year. In many parts of the County it was customary to collect large amounts of brush-wood and other materials on the last day of the year. They were used to make bonfires and lit about nine in the evening, kept going well into the morning of New Year's day. During the late nineteenth century the older Black Country folk would refuse to give a neighbour fire, or even a light from a candle, on the morning of New Year's Day. Many regarded their hearth fire as sacred at this time, and it was kept burning from twelve noon on New Year's Eve till midnight on New Year's day. If the fire went out, it was thought to be an omen that a member of the family would die during the year. The colliers refused to work on New Year's Eve and New Year's day, and it seems likely that their reasons for not working are closely related to the beliefs concerning the giving of fire and light and the sacredness of fire.

Unique to the County was the homage ceremony which fulfilled a feudal service owed by the Lord of Essington to the Lord of Hilton. Hilton Hall, Essington, near Wolverhampton, was once the home of an unusual figure known as Jack of Hilton. The figure, believed to be a fertility symbol of Etruscan origin, brought to Britain by the Romans, featured in the ceremony. Every New Year's day the Lord of Essington, or his bailiff, would bring a goose to Hilton Hall and drive it round the fire, 'at least three times whilst Jack of Hilton is blowing the fire'.

The hollow brass figure stands about one foot tall and is 'kneeling upon his left knee, and holding his Pego or veretum erected ...'. The figure has a small hole at the mouth about the size of a pin's head, and a hole at the back, two-thirds of an inch in diameter. Four and a quarter pints of water are poured through the hole into the figure which, 'when set to a strong fire, evaporates after the same manner as in an AEoliphile, and vents itself at the smaller hole at the mouth in a constant blast, blowing the fire so strongly that it is very audible, ... '

The Lord or his deputy then carried the goose to the kitchens where it was dressed. His final duty was to place the goose before the Lord of Hilton, when he received a dish of meat for his own table. Dr Robert Plot, who described the figure and its function in his *Natural History of Staffordshire,* saw it in use in May 1680, and learned from two brothers, Thomas and John a Stokes, that the custom had last taken place about fifty years previously, when they themselves had been present. Hilton Hall is now owned by a Catholic Order and is used as an old people's rest home. The figure was located in a private house in Wiltshire in November 1971.

Further north, at Abbots Bromley, it was customary to perform a Hobby Horse Dance on New Year's Day and Twelfth Day. Robert Plot describes the form of the dance, the characters and the props used in his *Natural History of Staffordshire.* Plot was writing in the 1680s when the tradition flourished, but no such dance was being performed by the end of the nineteenth century, according to various writers. Similar customs also took place at Stafford and Seighford, according to Plot. The dance involved the use of a figure of a horse, made from thin board and held between the legs, several pairs of red and white antlered horns, a bow and arrow and a spoon for collecting money. These were stored in the church tower under the care of the vicar and it seems likely they were the same props used in the famous Abbots Bromley Horn Dance, described in the September section.

The Hobby led the dancers with the horse between his legs. As he moved along, he twanged the bow; the arrow passed through a hole in the bow and stopped at the shoulder, making a snapping sound in time with the music. He was accompanied by six dancers carrying equal numbers of red and white reindeer antlers bearing the arms of the families of Paget, Bagot and Welles, the most prominent families in the area. Plot tells us that the Hobby dancers also owned:

a pot which was kept by turns by four or five of the chief of the town whom we call Reeves, who provided cakes and ale to put into this pot. All the people who had any kindness for the good interest of the institution of the sport, giving pence apiece for themselves and families, and so foreigners too, that came to see it; with which money the charge of the cakes and ale being defrayed, they not only repaired their church but kept their poor too; . . . .

The Hobby Horse dance was only one of the Twelfth Day observances in Staffordshire. Epiphany, 6 January, was also celebrated in other ways. Blount, the seventeenth-century antiquary, noted that: 'the inhabitants of Staffordshire make a fire on the Eve of Twelfth Day in memory of the blazing star that conducted the Three Magi to the manger at Bethlehem'.

Sometimes wassailing also took place on these occasions, as on New Year's Day. The Wassail might be accompanied by numerous short verses. The *Carroll for a Wassell-Bowl* was popular in Staffordshire and these verse extracts are from the version seen by the editor of *The Every-Day Book* at the printing office of Mr Rann of Dudley in 1819. The printer claimed that it was a popular piece with the Staffordshire and Warwickshire Wassailers:

A jolly Wassel-Bowl
A Wassell of good ale,
Well fare the butler's sole,
That setteth this to sale;
Our jolly Wassel

Good Dame, here at your door,
Our Wassell we begin,
We are all maidens poor,
We pray now let us in,
With our good Wassel.

Our Wassell we do fill
With apples and with spice,
They kindly will agree
To take a good carouse
Of our Wassel.

But here they let us stand
All freezing in the cold;
Goodmaster, give command,
To enter and be bold,
With our Wassel.

The wassailers continue to make entreaties arguing persuasively in favour of coming in. Having achieved their object, and pledged the Wassail, they sing:

And now we must be gone,
To seek out more good cheer,
Where bounty will be shown,
As we have found it here,
With our Wassel.

In Walsall the Eve of Twelfth Day signified the gift of a penny loaf, though each person was expected to fetch it. It was given to all those who lived in the town of Walsall, or in the outlying parish hamlets. According to local tradition, Thomas Moseley was riding through the town, when he heard a child crying for bread on the Eve of Epiphany. He resolved that such a distressing thing should never happen again. Accordingly he bestowed his manor of Bascote upon the town, to provide an annual penny loaf for every person within the liberties of Walsall on Twelfth Eve, for ever. This was known as the Moseley Dole.

Thomas Moseley did settle his manor at Bascote on the town, but only so that an Obit for the souls of himself and his wife might be performed in the church of Walsall and the Abbey of Hales Owen. The memorial service entitled the town to receive the rents of the manor and the bread dole appears to have been a discretionary payment from these rents. The first recorded instance was in 1539 when the bellman summoned the people to the church to pray for the souls of Thomas and Margaret Moseley; on this occasion the dole was given and £7 10s 9d (£7.54) was debited to that account. The dole flourished in Robert Plot's time, the late-seventeenth century, and, at a later date, it became customary to pay each inhabitant one penny, though this seems to have stopped after 1825.

Charles Poole, writing in the late nineteenth century, recalled that some Staffordshire villages still celebrated Plough Monday, the first Monday after Twelfth Day, and William Hone described the custom as practised early in the nineteenth century. He noted how the labourers would draw a plough and solicit money by guising and dancing with swords, preparatory to ploughing after the Christmas holiday. By the late-nineteenth century the plough was still processed, but the sword dancing had been omitted. In general the 'plough boys' dressed in colourful rags and tinsel.

Staffordshire seems to have been particularly noted for its Clogg Almanacs and, as these were a means of recording the annual festivals and customs, a brief account of their appearance and function is appropriate. The Cloggs were an ancient means of recording feasts, fasts and holidays and were generally carved from wood, though Robert Plot recalls seeing them in brass. They were squared sticks, varying from a few inches to a foot or more in length, and each side of the stick represents a quarter of the year. The days and weeks are notched into the appropriate side, and each seventh day is notched deeper and longer than the others to show the week divisions. Every remarkable day was then recorded by means of the carved symbols peculiar to the saint or event celebrated; these symbols were illustrative of the nature of the saint or event.

February

February customs, events and games centre round the moveable Lenten period. The forty days of lent, a period of confession and austerity, begin on Ash Wednesday and end on Easter day and, traditionally, the two preceding days are a time of festive pleasure – the final fling before Lent. The Monday that preceded Ash Wednesday was known throughout the county as Collop Monday, when it was customary to eat a dinner of meat collops, or bacon rashers, with eggs.

Shrove or Goodish Tuesday was not only celebrated, as it is today, by eating pancakes, but by a variety of means. The pancake bell, as it was known, was rung at 11am in many parish churches, to signify to the housewives that the preparation of the batter should begin. The children had good reason to celebrate Pancake Day, since it was common practice for a half day's holiday to be granted and the children chanted rhymes in honour of the pancake bell. In Bilston and Wednesbury they often accompanied the bell's ring with the rhyme:

> Ding-dong, pan on, ding-dong,
> Pull the big one off, put the little one on,
> Ding-dong, pan on, pan on, ding-dong!

This was commonly sung in the Black Country towns, but Wolverhampton children also chanted a rhyme for St Peter's Church:

> Pancakes and fritters,
> Say the bells of St Peter's!
> Let 'em fast who will,
> We'll have our fill.

Elsewhere each town had its bell rhyme, made round similar themes. At Wednesbury it ran:

> The pancake smells,
> Say the Wedgebury bells,
> Ding dong, ding dong,
> Ding dong, ding dong.

and at nearby Willenhall:

> Pan on, pan on,
> You can hear we miles,
> Say the bells of St. Gile's.
> The frying pan's on,
> And the pancake's done,
> Pan on.

Throughout the County the children would chant a rhyme to remind the school teachers of their right to a holiday:

> Pancake Day is a very happy day,
> If you don't give us holiday
> We'll all run away!

The first three pancakes were regarded as sacred. They were marked with a cross, sprinkled with salt to ward off evil, and then put aside. It might be that this rhyme was said over them:

> Good pancakes made of milk and beer
> Are made for no one present here;
> There's one for Peter, one for Paul,
> The third for Him who made us all.

At Stone it was customary to give the first pancake off to the fowl and, should it snow, the Black Country cooks would take the frying-pan outside to catch a few snow flakes; their addition to the batter was said to improve the flavour. In some areas the mid-day meal was made entirely of pancakes.

In parts of the County, including the Black Country, servants who 'lay-a-bed' on Shrove Tuesday had a pancake brought to their house. A crowd would gather and, if the person would not appear, the pancake was stuck onto the front door and left there as a mark of public shame at her idleness. Lawley, in his *Staffordshire Customs, Superstitions and Folklore* gives the following interesting description of the custom:

I remember seeing this curious custom put into practice in the year 1857. The pancake was carried on a plate by a middle-aged woman . . . . She was accompanied by all the 'ladies' of the locality who, as was their wont, castigated the unfortunate "lye-a-bed" with a cataract of offensive epithets, being encouraged to "keep it up" by a bodyguard of vagabond boys with tin cans, kettles and old pieces of iron, which they beat unmercifully with sticks, and added to the hubbub by shouting to the utmost capacity of their leathern lungs. On which occasion a riot nearly ensued through some of the "lye-a-bed's" acquaintances taking her part; during which hubbub the precious pancake disappeared . . .

This 'rough music' as it is known, was a traditional means of dealing with and shaming recalcitrants of various types. Shrove Tuesday marked the start of a number of outdoor games such as tip cat, marbles, skipping and hop-scotch, and many towns indulged in street football on this day. Plant, in his *History of Cheadle,* tells us that:

"Football was played on Shrove Tuesday in the main street of this town, when the shop-keepers put up their shutters, it being held that they had no remedy for broken windows on that day."

The games often involved parish against parish or, alternatively, one part of a town against another. In the Black Country the two o'clock or 'football bell' was rung to announce the games commencement and the two teams mustered their ranks. The teams consisted of the greater number of the able-bodied inhabitants, and the ball was placed at the half-way spot, both teams endeavouring to get the ball to their own end.

At Lichfield Grammar School the traditional practice of 'barring out' the masters flourished during the late seventeenth century, though records after this date are scant. The custom was popular at many schools, including Bromfield School, Eaton, on Shrove Tuesday and in some cases the masters were forced to remain out of school for two or three days.

An adult sport particularly associated with Shrove Tuesday was throwing at cocks; it was widely practised in Staffordshire, as it was in many other regions, until the early 19th century, but instances are rare after this time. Lawley describes the South Staffordshire version thus:

A stake was driven in an open space of ground, to which stake a cord was attached at one end. The other was tied to the cock's leg, giving him some ten feet of loose cord to enable him to dodge the missiles of his persecutors. At a distance of 22 yards another post was driven in, at which the thrower stood. The charge for throwing was two pence for three shies. If the thrower knocked the bird down and caught it before it recovered, he took it as his prize. If he failed, he gave place to another thrower. Broom handles or staves cut to a length of three feet were the weapons used. The excitement consisted in the agility of the bird in eluding the missiles (to which purpose he was carefully trained) and to the skill of the thrower. Some of the birds were astonishingly agile and knowing, their quick eye enabling them to gauge fairly accurately where the stave would fall. Some birds would escape unharmed for hours, so that a clever cock would bring much money into the owner's pocket. Like many other cruel sports it frequently ended in disturbances and free fights.

The same account details events that occurred in 1790 at Bilston, told by an old resident of that town. On this occasion the cock was particularly agile and, eventually, an enraged contestant rushed at it and wrung its neck, before the owner could intervene. This led to a general free for all, and only ended when the magistrate and constable arrived; several of the brawlers were fined for their part in the affray.

March

Collop Monday and Shrove Tuesday are moveable feasts that not infrequently occur in early March, but the month is particularly associated with Mothering Sunday and the customs surrounding it. The day was marked by eating certain food and by visits home to pay respects to parents, particularly mother. Such visits are still a common feature of modern Mother's Day and it is also accepted that a Mother's Day card should be sent together with flowers or a small gift; children and husbands often prepare the family meals on the day and relieve mother of most of her normal household jobs. Traditionally her wishes and requests are observed and the day revolves round her.

Of course it is important not to confuse the two events. Traditional Mothering Sunday was celebrated on the fourth Sunday in Lent, also known as Mid-Lent Sunday. Before the Reformation it was a time for visiting the Mother Church of the parish to attend a service. In time it came to be associated with the idea of honouring one's own mother, a custom popular by the time of Herrick in the seventeenth century, for he wrote:

> I'll to thee a Simnell bring
> 'Gainst thou go'st a mothering
> So that, when she blesseth thee,
> Half that blessing thou'lt give me.

Modern Mother's Day is observed on the second Sunday in May. Thanks to the efforts of a Miss Anna Jarvis of Philadelphia, the American Congress recognized it as an official festival in 1914, and it was introduced into England by American soldiers stationed here during the Second World War.

During the nineteenth century Mothering Sunday was observed with a variety of special foods. At Draycot-in-the-Moors and surrounding villages the fourth Sunday in Lent was also known as Fig Pie Wake and special pies made of dry-figs, sugar, treacle and spice were cooked and set aside. Any visitor expected and received a piece of wake pie. At Stone and Eccleshall and other north county towns the traditional mid-day meal consisted of roast veal and custard – the same food was still being eaten in the 1930s in the Wolverhampton area – and it was sometimes served with a sauce made from salt fish and eggs. This meal was eaten at Wednesbury in South Staffordshire, where the custard pudding was baked in layers with various fruits and other ingredients and thought to be a great delicacy; it was known as 'laid pudding' because of the layering. The most famous Black Country dish – known of course in other parts of the country too – was 'frumity' or 'frumenty'. G. T. Lawley's *Staffordshire Customs, Superstitions and Folklore* tells us:

It was a custom in Staffordshire at harvest time, when the corn was 'inned' or garnered, for women and girls to go into the fields to glean the scattered ears of corn for the purpose of making up into miniature sheaves, which they hung on the rafters of their dwellings where they remained in readiness for Mothering Sunday, when they were taken down, the grains soaked in water for several hours, and being well creed they were put into a stew-pot, and stewed till quite soft, when, with the addition of milk, sugar or treacle, they became a standing dish on that day, under the name of "frumity", or properly "frumenty" of which everyone partook at the Sunday dinner.

Lawley records that the custom was common in his childhood during the mid-nineteenth century. He had encountered the custom of hanging sheaves ready for Mothering Sunday in a house in Wednesbury, during the 1880s.

A less expensive dish, often eaten by the poorer families, consisted of dried grey peas and bacon, which were stewed together and eaten as a substitute for frumenty. The Black Country rhyme, extolling the virtues of grey peas and bacon ran:

> Peas and bacon in a pot
> Stewed till they be tender got;
> Served up in a trencher wide
> To match the room in yo're inside,
> Bin very good for hungry men
> When Motherin' Sunday comes agen.

The dish, commonly pronounced grey *pays* and bacon, is now a popular speciality throughout South Staffordshire and is regarded as a typical local dish. The Mothering Sunday meal might well have been rounded off with 'Mothering Cakes', as they were called in Staffordshire, or Simnel cakes, as they were known in Shropshire. There is a legend that the name Simnel derives from an old Shropshire couple, Sim and Nell, who were in dispute whether the mixture for the Mothering Sunday cake should be boiled or baked. Sim said it should be boiled and Nell vice versa. Their argument led to a fight with besoms and brooms. Eventually they compromised and the cake was first part-boiled and then part-baked to complete the job; since that time it became the traditional method of preparing it. Simnels were often given to parents during the annual visit.

Of all the various dinners and puddings associated with Mothering Sunday, the most highly thought of in South Staffordshire seems to have been 'raist beef and laid'; as famous and popular as the

traditional Christmas turkey. The 'laid' consisted of milk, gravy from
the roast beef and a light batter, the whole being left in the pan until
the joint had cooked. The result was a golden brown pudding not
unlike a Yorkshire pudding, with a 'delicate' flavour, the result of
cooking in an open pan over a good fire.

In an industrial area like the Black Country it is not surprising to
find a Mothering Sunday custom practised by the local miners. G. T.
Lawley describes it in his *Staffordshire Customs, Superstitions and
Folklore:* 'In the Black Country it was once the custom for butty
colliers to give a toast ale to all the men employed at their pits, and
to feast their apprentices with beans and bacon.' The butty colliers
were the mining middlemen, who leased the mine-workings from the
owners, and hired the colliers.

At one time the Monday following Mothering Sunday was known
as Fathering Monday. Although there were no special customs or
foods associated with this day, father was treated with solicitous
respect and the family gathered to continue the fun of the previous
day. Dinner was usually cold remains of the Mothering Sunday meal.
In the early nineteenth century, when Fathering Day was still
observed, this wise rhyme was widely known in Staffordshire:

> If in Lent you borrow
> You'll find out to your sorrow
> You'll be worse off to-morrow.

It was also customary to mark the sixth Sunday in Lent, Palm
Sunday, by the custom of decorating the church with branches of
'English Palms', especially box, yew, or willow – which was much
sought after, if it bore catkins. This practice was still maintained in
some Staffordshire parishes in the early twentieth century, and in a
modified form continues today. At St Michael and All Angels, the
parish church in Tettenhall, Wolverhampton, the vicar leads the
congregation in procession; he carries a sheaf of real palm leaves,
though these are imported from the East. The church is decorated
with other palm sheaves about the altar, and the congregation receive
pieces of palm made up in the form of a cross; these should be kept
until the following Ash Wednesday and then burnt. In the late
nineteenth century many Protestant Staffordshire miners flocked to
the Catholic Church to obtain palms for use in the mines as charms
against the devil.

April

April 1st or All Fools' Day, as it is universally known, is still a vigorous custom in Staffordshire as it is elsewhere in England. Young and old endeavour to play as many tricks and practical jokes on each other as they can, though it is generally agreed that these games should stop at twelve noon; according to one or two nineteenth-century historians the whole day was set aside for 'fooling' at one time.

The greater number of April customs and beliefs revolve round Easter, and Good Friday was an occasion for various observances. The colliers of South Staffordshire refused to work then, because they believed some great disaster would befall them; in previous times all work ceased on Good Friday and no doubt the colliers' attitude stemmed from this. Perhaps their need for a day's holiday arose from the general practice of starting the garden patch on Good Friday, since many Black Country workmen liked to spend the whole day working on their allotments, digging, sowing and planting out. In the house their wives would not dispose of soapsuds in the gutter on Good Friday or Easter Monday, for fear of bringing bad luck to the family. Indeed many would not throw out soapsuds until Easter Tuesday, and only then with reluctance. The special holiness of Good Friday gave certain everyday jobs a special potency: 'It is fairly well known that a belief exists that home-made ointment manufactured on Good Friday from constituents in which lard plays an important part will cure sores of long standing in twenty-four hours after application ...' Likewise, bread baked on Good Friday, filled with quick silver, and placed in water, would immediately float to the spot directly above a dead body.

Perhaps the best known Good Friday custom is the baking and eating of hot cross buns. The rhymes chanted by the children included:

> One a penny buns,
> Two a penny buns,
> One a penny, two a penny,
> Hot cross buns.

> Hot cross buns,
> Two for Peter, one for Paul,
> And three for Him who made us all
> Hot cross buns.

and

> One a penny poker,
> Two a penny tongues,
> Three a penny fire shovels
> Hot cross buns.

These rhymes could be heard frequently in late nineteenth-century Staffordshire, when the buns were eaten with afternoon tea rather than at any other time of day. As recently as 1949 the children of Christ Church Primary School at Tettenhall Wood, Wolverhampton, were chanting their version of the hot cross bun rhyme:

> Hot cross buns, hot cross buns,
> One a penny, two a penny
> Hot cross buns.
> If you have no daughters give them to your sons,
> One a penny, two a penny
> Hot cross buns.

At Christ Church school it was customary for the children to line up in the early afternoon to receive their hot cross buns, which were handed out from a large metal tray; once they had received their buns, they were allowed to go home early.

The buns were marked with a cross, and it was also believed that a loaf of bread baked on Good Friday from a leaven marked with a cross would stay fresh and edible until the following Easter. The same bread, grated into warm beer or tea, became a cure-all for stomach pains. Those whose stomach pains proved too strong for this traditional remedy might obtain relief from cramps and fits by wearing a hallowed ring as a charm against such ailments; these rings were blessed by the priest and given to sufferers. Beside hot cross buns, stewed grey peas and bacon was a special Good Friday dish in South Staffordshire. It was cooked in most of the public houses and given away to the customers.

The widespread custom of pace-egging was also practiced in the county in the early nineteenth century and is described in an account written at the beginning of this century:

> Towards the close of the day a group of young men and women
> of the peasant class in strange and ludicrous disguise would

indulge in what was known as "paste egging." They would go to the houses of the well-to-do and solicit gifts of eggs, oatcakes, and money, to enable them the better to celebrate the festival of Easter. Many of the eggs thus collected were in the interval between Good Friday and Easter Day coloured and ornamented, and sold as Easter eggs at a considerable profit.

It was commonly believed in the Black Country that the sun danced on Easter Sunday. So firm was this belief that large crowds gathered in the early morning and stood staring into the east to see this phenomenon; a number of writers recalled seeing such gatherings during the late nineteenth century and early twentieth century. Many claimed to have seen the dance take place; it was thought to occur because of Christ's Ascension.

Churches were lavishly decorated on Easter Sunday with the usual boughs of birch, willow, palm, box, and broom, together with all the flowers in bloom at that time of the year and, in addition, many South Staffordshire churches added various religious figures and a large number of wax candles. Decorating churches is still common in Staffordshire, but the custom of 'clipping the church' seems to have disappeared some time during the early nineteenth century. G. T. Lawley, in his *Staffordshire Customs, Superstitions and Folklore*, tells us that:

In the Black Country it was customary at Easter for the children of the parish schools to "clip the church". The children were assembled in the schoolroom and marshalled by the beadle and other parish officers, in procession, and then proceed to the church. When the head of the procession arrived there, the first child turned her back to the building, the second then took her right hand and so every child in succession until the building was surrounded, when they sang the hymn commencing "Round about Thy Temple, Lord". The procession then reformed and was marched back to the schoolroom, where they were regaled with tea and buns and after that engaged in simple and harmless amusements.

In many regions it was customary to roll eggs down grassy slopes on Easter Monday, while in Staffordshire and other Midland Counties the young boys and girls rolled themselves down grassy slopes, racing each other to the bottom. At Wednesbury, the favourite spot was an open space called The Mounts, where the practice took place until 1830, but is not recorded after that date. The most popular Easter Custom, without doubt, was 'Heaving'. This event took place on Monday and Tuesday, generally known as the 'Heaving Days', and is reported from many parts of Staffordshire.

On Monday the men would 'heave' the women and on Tuesday vice-versa. Between the hours of 9.00 am and twelve noon bands of men and women roved the streets of the towns and villages looking for 'victims'. When an unsuspecting person was spotted, they gave chase, or lay in wait to pounce upon their prey, who was lifted three times into the air and had to kiss each of the men or pay a silver forfeit; in the case of the women, they expected a kiss from the man and a silver forfeit. The means of lifting varied from area to area and depended upon the nature of the person lifted. Some were chaired above, others lifted bodily by one person, others taken hold of by arms and legs and flung aloft. The custom was particularly vigorous in the early part of the nineteenth century when the excitable, unkempt, vociferous, and sometimes drunken band of 'heavers' became the subjects of adverse comment from the press and officialdom.

In any discussion of Easter practices in Staffordshire the singing of Easter carols must be mentioned. The West Midlands was an extremely important area for carols, and some of the finest versions have been collected in the region. Easter carols are less common than their Christmas counterparts, but the custom of singing Easter carols was still observed in the 1880s, when *The Jews they Crucified Him,* or *The Gornal Nailmakers' Carol,* was noted down from a nailmaker in the industrial village of Gornal. The Gornal version was taken down in words only and this is how it is given here, though it might be added that Cecil Sharp collected tunes for the carol in the United States of America, and Peter Kennedy obtained a version complete with tune from a gypsy in Herefordshire:

The Jews they Crucified Him

The Jews they crucified Him,
O, the Jews they crucified Him,
O, the Jews they crucified Him,
And nailed Him to a tree!

Mary stood a-weeping,
Mary stood a-weeping,
Mary stood a-weeping,
To see the Lord a-bleeding.

Then Joseph begged the body,
Then, etc.
And laid it in a tomb.

Came down then an angel,
Came, etc.
And rolled away the stone.

And then up rose the Saviour,
And then, etc.
To conquer Death and Hell!

Then tell John, James and Peter,
Then tell, etc.
I'm risen from the dead!

The eternal gates were open,
The eternal, etc.
To let our Saviour in!

Our last April custom is St George's Court, which is held at the
Guild Hall, Lichfield, on 23 April, though it may be moved to the
22nd if the 23rd falls on a Sunday. The Town Clerk, as Steward of
the Manor, presides over the Court, which meets at twelve noon and
lasts between one and two hours. A jury, which is chosen at random,
hears complaints and the Court appoints a Bailiff, two High Constables, two Commoners, two Pinlock Keepers, and seven Dozeners.
Anciently the Commoners took care of the common lands, the
Pinlock Keepers tended the stray animal pound, and the Dozeners
maintained general order in the ward of the city assigned to them.
St George's Court combines two courts. The Court of the View of
Frankpledge and the Court Baron of the Manor of Lichfield. At the
first, male subjects of fourteen years swore allegiance to the King;
the second was a customary court applying to copyholders, and also
a common-law court.

May

May is an active month in the Staffordshire calendar and events get under way at the earliest possible date with the local May Day celebrations. Maying was still popular in the mid-nineteenth century and Lawley, a local historian, described the events among Black Country colliers and other people living in the Bilston district in about 1850:

> A few years ago we saw a modern exhibition of this ancient May Day revelry in this district. It was usual fifty years ago for colliers out of work, or on strike to go in bands of about a dozen, decorated with ribbons, and armed with stout staves, accompanied by a fiddler, to the sound of whose music the band went through a curious kind of dance. The men stood opposite each other in groups of four, and, at a particular part of the tune, struck each other's staves one, two, three, crossing from side to side as they did so, ... The dancers all wore ribbons in their caps, as did also the man with the collecting-box, which was fastened at the end of a long stick, and occasionally received a vigorous shaking, as a spur to the liberality of the crowd, or as an accompaniment to the music. Others of the villagers wreathed the garlands for the maypole dance, constructed the rustic framework for the bower of the Queen of the May, and made preparations for the coming feast. When the wanderers returned from the greenwood, they cast their trophies on the village green, ... until all had returned, when the choicest boughs were selected for the vantages of honour, and then adorned with ribbons, gay handkerchiefs, and bits of personal finery were hung up, some over the doors of the village mansions, some over the lintels of the ancient hostelry, some in the church porch, ...

The tallest of these boughs was selected as the may-pole and erected on the green, having been decorated with streamers and garlands. Sometimes the maypole underwent a christening ceremony: the village 'crier' poured part of a pot of 'humming ale' over it and drank the remainder. The ceremony is referred to in the following rhyme obtained from an old Bilstonian by G. T. Lawley:

Up with the maypole, high let it be,
If none say me 'Nay!' I'll now christen thee,
The maypole, the maypole, thy name it shall be,
Now all you good folk, come shout with me
                                    Hurrah! Hurrah!

Close by, at Wolverhampton, a party of mayers recited a local
maypole rhyme that describes the actual jaunt round the may-pole:

All round the maypole we will trot,
From the very bottom to the very top;
        Now I've got my Nancy
        To trundle on my knee.
        Oh! my lovely Nancy
        She's the girl for me.
        She hops and she skips
        While the tabors play,
        It's well for the shepherds
        On the first of May.
        First come the buttercups,
        Then come the daisies,
        Then come the gentles,
        Then come the ladies;
So all around the maypole here we trot,
From the very bottom to the very top.

In the 1850s the colliers and ironworkers of the Black Country,
along with various other workmen, would visit the countryside on
May Day to take the customary whey drink. The drink was a
combination of rum and milk; the rum they took with them and the
milk was obtained from local farmhouses. They drank in honour of
the day and 'the country lanes, public houses and fields, used to be
covered with these whey-drinking parties, who in their noisy half
drunken condition ran races, fought pitched battles, . . . and made
havoc wherever they went, leaving desolation behind, ...

The workers also decorated pit-frames, engine-houses, chimney-
stacks and iron-works with may-boughs and blossoms, but most of
these activities appear to have died out by the end of the nineteenth
century, when only the odd may-bough was seen in the iron-works.

At this time it was still customary in various parts of the county to decorate horses with ribbons and bows. In Uttoxeter the children carried garlands of may flowers through the town, calling at various houses, where they were given small amounts of money. The larger garlands consisted of two hoops, one passed through the other, which were wound round with evergreen boughs and flowers, and capped with a bunch of flowers. In the centre of the hoops was hung a pendant orange, surrounded with flowers. Individual children would carry a stick with blooms tied to it, and the children decorated themselves with ribbons and flowers.

Accounts of the hobby horse dancing and mumming that once took place as part of Staffordshire's May Day celebrations are fairly common. The mummers and morris dancers welcomed in the spring. The chief characters were Jack-in-the-Green and his wife, attended by a variety of dancers, dressed in rags and decorated with tinsel. As they capered, through the town they collected money in a box. Jack's 'wife' carried it and he danced alongside, covered in may-boughs, ribbons and tinsel. Very often the dancers were the town chimney-sweeps: as elsewhere, this was part of the tradition. Prior to the Restoration of Charles II, Stafford churches paid for repairs from the proceeds of the May Day hobby horse dance. The dancing procession was attended by the traditional hobby, who 'sat' astride a stick topped with a horse's head; he led the dancers to the sound of pipes and tabors. The Stafford dance took place on 12 May.

In many places the local squire provided a May feast and the Fool, belonging to the band of mummers, was given fill licence to carry out various tricks and pranks to amuse the company. The toast at such feasts varied, but that used at Wednesbury ran:

> Here's a health to the merry month,
> The merry month of May;
> Drink deep, and pledge it in a cup,
> To drive dull care away.
> Pledge it all, both great and small,
> Pledge it now, come one and all,
>   Hurray, hurray, hurray!

May Day was a free and easy time, but those who visited the homes of others did well to remember that taking may-boughs into a house uninvited brought bad luck to the household. Marrying in May was also ill-omened. May dew, however, possessed magical qualities. Those girls who got up early enough to collect it from the woods and bathe their faces with it, believed it would give them great beauty.

'Beating the Bounds', as it was called, used to occur during Rogation week and preceded the moveable feast of Ascension, which takes place from 30 April at the earliest, to 3 June at the latest. This perambulation of the parish boundaries was carried out by officers of the church and the civil authorities, who were usually accompanied by large numbers of parishioners. The annual processioning took place with great regularity in many Staffordshire towns until the end of the eighteenth century; processioning occurred after this time but on a sporadic basis. In the bigger towns it might take three days to complete the circuit; the Gospel was read at various landmarks along the route. Many of these boundary markers were trees, often oaks, which were known as 'Gospel trees', because of the custom of reading the Gospel beneath them. One of the boundary-markers on the Wolverhampton route was an oak, as we learn from the account of the perambulation in 1823, given in the church books for 1824:

From thence we proceeded across the road leading from Wolverhampton to Cannock, down a lane on the left-hand side to Featherstone; where, under an oak tree in the road, near to the house now occupied by Mr. William Price, the Gospel was read a fifth and last time for this day.

The situation of the boundary markers was often a matter of folk memory and it was not unusual to find that the parish clerk had remembered the spot with the help of various customary devices. Lawley writes:

Last week we gave an instance of a man named Walter Gough, who was thrown into a bed of nettles by the parish clerk of Wolverhampton, to impress the parish boundary upon his mind. The incident was not by any means an unusual one in connection with these parochial perambulations. It was customary at particular spots to bump a boy's seat of honour against a boundary stone or tree, or to throw another one into a brook or pool, or to beat a third one with hazel switches, to impress the boundary upon the memory the more deeply. Sometimes an aged parishioner was carried with the processioners and at certain points his evidence of the boundary marks was taken down in the presence of witnesses, and duly deposited in the parish chest . . . for further reference.

This technique of recording the boundary-markers was not common in Staffordshire. The method used by the parish clerk to remember the boundary also served to sharpen the memory of the young children who attended the processioning; particularly the unfortunates who suffered the custom, since they would be expected to carry it on later in life. At Lichfield, where the event took place only once in seven years because of the expense, the need for such reminders was even greater. Apart from this, it seems to have been customary to obtain the word of those who had been 'bumped', or who had touched the marker on previous occasions, as to the accuracy of the boundary. Their word was used to reinforce the written accounts that were generally made of each perambulation, even though the accounts gave fairly detailed descriptions of the various markers.

At Leek, in North Staffordshire, May was a particularly busy month. Apart from the usual monthly celebrations, the town had been granted a May Fair and Court of Pie Powder following an inquisition at Stafford: after the inquisition, which took place on 10 June 1629, Charles I granted the rights on 14 July of the same year to:

Thomas Jodderile, gentleman, his heirs and assigns, full and absolute licence, liberty, power, advantage and authority to have, hold and keep within the said Manor and Village of Leek and the precincts thereof, one Fair or Market yearly for ever, on the 7th, 8th, and 9th days of May yearly, to be held and kept for all those days to continue, together with a Court of Pie Powder there at the time of the said Fair or Market aforesaid, and with all liberty and free Customes, Tolls, Stallage, Pickage, Fines, Amerceiaments, and all other profits, commodities, and emoluments whatsoever to a Fair or Market of that sort and to a Court of Pie Powder belonging, happening, contingent, or in any manner appertaining.

The Court of Pie Powder, also known as 'Dusty-foot Court', was held during the fair to dispense justice to buyers and sellers, and to redress wrongs committed at the fair. 'Pickage' was a term used to denote the cash paid at a fair for the preparation of the ground prior to setting up the stalls. Leek still has its May fair, which is held roundabout 8 May, though it is now essentially a pleasure fair.

Staffordshire is very closely associated with Charles II's escape from the Roundhead soldiers, so it is not surprising that Oak Apple Day on 29 May was a popular celebration in the county. In 1660, 29 May was officially appointed as a day of thanksgiving, and from this date local church records include items of expenditure relating to the Royal Oak or Restoration Day activities:

WOLVERHAMPTON	s.	d.	
1663—Given to ye ringers on May ye 29th for ringing in honour of his blessed Majestie's most gracious restoration	3	0	(15p)

DARLASTON			
1807—For drink at Foster's for ye ringers on May ye 29th	5	0	(25p)

On the morning of the 29th those who lived in the locality made an early start, visiting the various places with which Charles was closely associated, beginning with Bentley Hall, then Moseley, Chillington, and Boscobel, where it was customary to have oak leaf decorations and spend the day at various sports and other amusements. School children wore a piece of oak, and those caught without their piece were beaten with stinging nettles, hence the day was also called 'nettling day'. It was generally a holiday in Staffordshire and many school boys played out a mock battle of Royalists and Roundheads. Equal numbers of boys met on the village green, half of them wearing hats decorated with oak leaves. The battle, known as the Royal Oak Fight, then took place under the supervision of a master. The contestants would pair off, one boy mounting another's back, and the two teams would fight with wooden lances and swords. The fight was arranged to turn out in favour of of the Royal Oak party; the leader of the group was crowned with an oak garland by the schoolmaster, and referred to as King Charles for the remainder of the day.

May 29th was widely celebrated at the beginning of the nineteenth century and in many communities was given pride of place over May Day. In the villages and hamlets people decorated specially erected poles with flowers, the lanes were hung with garlands, and everyone wore oak leaves in their hats. Music and dancing took place on the village greens, and many went to Boscobel to inspect the hiding places used by Charles II after his flight from the Battle of Worcester in 1651; the trip was a particular favourite with Black Country people.

Perhaps the most universal of the May celebrations was Whitsun, still an important holiday in the county, as it is throughout the country. It was generally the custom to decorate churches, homes and various other buildings in towns and villages with blossoms and foliage from the countryside, and the accounts in many Staffordshire Church Registers contain items relating to church decoration:

ST LEONARD'S BILSTON   s. d.

1692—For dressing ye chapell with birch att
   Whitsuntide   6 (2½p)
1694—To Anne Knowles for cleaning and
   dressing ye chapell att Whitsuntide 2 0 (10p)

Whitsun weekend, and particularly Whit Monday, was given over to feasting, drinking, attending fairs and participating in various sports. The Whitsun Ale, as it was known, was provided by the churches. They churchwardens purchased or received gifts of malt, which they brewed into beer and sold in the church or churchyard, the money going to the support of the poor and the maintenance of the church. During these Church Ales the public houses remained closed under pain of a statutory fine. The Whitsun Ale generally started after the morning service, and it was not unusual for the church wardens to hire musicians for the occasion. Where the population of a parish was likely to be too great for the space available at the church, other means were adopted:

The church wardens had to secure a large farmer's barn, which was plentifully adorned with branches of birch, willow, and box, bunches of flowers, and parti-coloured ribbons, and filled with benches. A dais was erected at one end for the lord and lady of the drinking, the parson, churchwardens and squire. Two persons of repute were chosen at a vestry meeting to take the part of the lord and lady of the ale, who had their necessary officers and suite; including a fool whose duty it was to make sport for the assembly. ... All these fellows were dressed in finery, such as parti-coloured garments, gay ribbons, the gown being provided with the usual Cockscomb and bauble.

The ale was brought in great leathern bottles which were put under the control of a steward who was fat as fat beseemed, with a white apron across his ample paunch ....

In the churchyard, or near the barn, Robin Hood's bower was erected for Robin Hood and his archers, represented by various villagers. They remained in their bower, until the time came for them to withdraw to the shooting butts, where they took part in a shooting competition for the silver arrow. This was a competition encouraged by order of the Tudor monarchs.

During the day the morris dancers and mummers were called on to perform their dances and play their set-piece with the characters of Robin Hood, Maid Marion, Hobby Horse, and the Bishop of Marham, who replaced the stock character of Friar Tuck at the Whitsun Ale. The dances were accompanied by pipe and tabor and these same characters performed the Whitsun dance, which began in slow measured tread and ended in an orgy of wild movement and shouting. When the dance had come to an end, the assembled company sang the Whitsun song:

> Now be the merry Whitsun come
>   Sing oh, sing hillo;
> Bring out tabor, bring out drum,
>   Heigh ho, heigh ho!
> Arbours for the maidens,
>   Alleys for the men,
> While the bells are ringing,
>   Whitsun's come again.
>   Sing, sing, heigh ho!

Many of these activities had gone into decline by the end of the eighteenth century and had virtually disappeared by the end of the nineteenth.

Today Whitsun is an important holiday for Staffordshire folk, though, with the exception of some revival morris dancing in places like Wolverhampton, the activities are likely to centre round race-meetings, family visits to seaside and countryside, and similar outings.

Staffordshire's main Whitsun Monday events are the Lichfield Greenhill or Whitsun Bower, and the Court of Array; two obser-vances which were once separate customs, but now form part of a single gathering.

The Greenhill Bower had its origins in a medieval trade fair and is so called because it took place on Greenhill, where bowers were erected for the display of local craftsman-made goods. More anciently it may derive from a flower festival. The Court of Array derives from the yearly inspection of military equipment laid down by the Statute of Westminster in 1285, which confirmed and formalised earlier laws and acts, such as that of 1176. The Statute laid down that every man between the ages of fifteen and sixty years should provide a stated weight of armour, according to the quantity of their lands and goods.

Today the Bower festivities are organised by a Bower Committee, consisting of people with an interest in the Bower.

The Court of Array still convenes in the Guild Hall on Whit Monday morning, and at 11.30 am the Mayor, Sheriff and Court Steward enter the Court. The Steward declares the Court open, reads an historical account of the custom and its significance, and calls upon the High Constable to receive the reports of the Dozeners who, historically, were appointed to keep the King's peace and inspect military equipment. Finally, the High Constable makes his report to the Lord of the Manor (the Mayor) and the Court is closed. The participants take light refreshments and join the carnival procession, which starts from Cherry Orchard, just outside the City centre. The procession starts at twelve noon and passes the Guild Hall between 12.30 pm and 1.00 pm, where it is joined by the Mayor and other Court Officials. It circuits the town, taking in Greenhill, and returns to Cherry Orchard, where it disperses. Traditionally the streets were garlanded with ribbons, boughs and flags and the morris dancers, eight, not six in number, played an extensive part in the proceedings. The dancers no longer took part after 1884 but today, following one or two abortive revivals, the Lichfield Morris is again a feature of the festival.

For a number of reasons Greenhill is now little used for the festivities of the Bower. The major celebrations take place at Beacon Park where, on Whit Monday afternoon, a huge sports meeting is organised and marquees are set up to provide food and drink. The sports meeting features an unusual item, steer-riding, which has been popular during the last two years. In the town itself two fun-fairs are in full swing; a small one in Market Square, and a larger one in a town-centre car park. Streets in the city centre are closed to traffic during the celebrations. Particular details of time and place for the events change from year to year, and intending visitors should check with the Town Hall.

At one time well-dressing was extremely common in Staffordshire; Milton, Uttoxeter, Billbrook, Blymhill, Burton-on-Trent, Brewood, West Bromwich and Endon were some of the places that held regular and flourishing well-dressing ceremonies. By the end of the 19th century the custom had largely disappeared from Staffordshire and, at the present time, Endon is the only village in the county to continue with its well-dressing.

Endon began the custom in 1845 and in 1868 the crowning of a well-dressing queen was added to the event. The present-day method of well-dressing is said to date back a mere one hundred and fifty years or so, though its origins are believed to lie in pagan worship of water gods and spirits. The custom takes place annually during Spring Bank Holiday Monday, although the preparations are lengthy and fairly complex. The dressings are fashioned on trays of varying sizes which, when complete, are suspended from a plank framework over the well. The bottom of the tray may be covered with parallel laths, drilled with half-inch holes, or covered with nails projecting a quarter of an inch or so; the tray is then coated with moist clay. Sketches of the required scene are drawn on large sheets of paper, and these are placed face upwards on the clay, while picture outlines are cut or pricked onto the clay beneath. The sheets are kept for reference and the outline is then boldened by pressing tiny alder cones, rhubarb seeds, or some other small hard seeds into the clay. This work is started a good week before the event, since it takes quite some time to create the floral picture. The first parts made are those that will not fade quickly, like roads and walls, which are picked out in bark, moss, lichen, cones and similar materials. There follows a massive gathering of blooms and then the craftsmen and women can begin their work; today the blooms tend to be cultured rather than wild. The flowers are sometimes used whole, with the remains of the stalk pressed into the clay, but most of the petals are placed with their edges sticking into the clay. The pictures are usually worked from the bottom and overlapped like roof slates, so that they shed the rain.

The best time to see a dressed well is as soon as possible after completion, since the blooms tend to fade and the dressing loses its lustre within a very short time.

Endon's well-dressing has now become a sizeable event, attracting many thousands of visitors; to cater for them, there is a fun-fair, morris dancing, various events and side-shows and a competitive farming custom, known as 'Tossing the Sheaf' – sheaves of corn are flung over a moveable cross-bar, slung between two poles. The Well-Dressing Queen ceremony is regarded as an important part of the event. She is crowned four times in all: on Saturday afternoon following the church service, early Saturday evening, and twice on Monday. The Well-Dressing Committee is chosen by open election in the village.

There are few tales that involve well-dressing, but a story once told on the Staffordshire—Derbyshire border describes how an old woman, who lived in a lonely cottage, managed to win the local well-dressing competition with the help of a hob. The old lady lived by herself and, assisted by the farmer who owned her cottage, managed to feed, clothe and shelter herself. However she always wished for 'a bit of company' and, like many households of the area, would put a bowl of milk porridge and a bit of cake on the doorstep before going to bed; this was provided for 'the luck', thought to be a hob, a small, friendly individual. On one occasion she found the food had been eaten and shortly after this she heard a strange voice calling out:

> Oh dear oh,
> Where can I go,
> In rain and snow?

Oh dear oh,
What can I do?
Let me come in
And stay with you.

The old woman, known for her kindness and good temper, thought quickly who it might be; a ghost perhaps or even Summat Else. Still she felt it needed company and bravely called it to come in, pointing out that it was welcome, even though the fire was low and food was short. A brown hand came round the door, followed by the rest of Summat Else, and she saw the small, brown creature slip along the wall and jump up into the chimney. She closed the door and climbed into bed, muttering that the fire was too low and the creature would be cold. Half-way through the night, she awoke to find a roaring fire in the grate and the smell of baking filling the house. She saw porridge bubbling on the stove, two brown cakes standing ready to eat, and a neat stack of dry turves ready for the fire. She divided the porridge and the cakes, eating her portion and putting the remainder in the grate for the hob.

She slept in next morning and was woken by the farmer. He had come to collect a rosebud for his wife, who was attending the village well-dressing. The farmer said it was a pity the old woman could not make a dressing above her well, but she lived too far out and was not fit enough to collect all the petals that were needed. The old woman went back into the house, wishing that she could dress her well but realising that it was impossible. When she closed the door she found to her surprise that the fire had been blown up again and her breakfast was waiting for her on the table. She ate the meal and then decided to go out and pick a few flowers as a token dressing for the rock above the well. She opened the door and the cottage was flooded with the scent of freshly-picked flowers. She thought the smell came from the local manor house but, looking up the garden, saw a huge pile of flower petals by her spring. She cried out with joy and set to work to finish her dressing before the church bell rang, even though she knew that the judges would not pass that way. She finished just in time and, as the bells started to ring, she heard voices coming along the lane. The farmer had brought the judges that way, so that the old woman could see them. The judges saw the beautiful arrangement of flowers and went on their way.

They returned in the evening to tell her that she had been awarded the first prize of three silver pennies; the new young squire, who thought his dressing would win first prize, had given the judges lunch and returned to London in a huff because the old woman had won. Just before the well-dressing, the squire had given the porridge and cake that his servants had put out for 'the luck' to his dogs. By doing this he had rejected 'the luck' and brought trouble to his household.

Delighted with her good fortune, the old woman went back into her cottage to find that, once again, all her chores had been done and the food was ready in front of a roaring fire. She sat down to her supper saying to herself, 'How lucky I am. Here I sit with Food and Fire and Company. Thank you kindly, whoever you are.'

June

In June the only date of significance was Midsummer Eve. In the south of the county it was believed that all the witches on earth gathered on the moon for 'The Witches Parliament' on Midsummer Night, where they arranged the fate of ordinary mortals for the next year. The date was of great importance to Staffordshire folk and, until the early nineteenth century, it gave rise to a number of customs, beliefs and practices. The day began early with the collection of flowers and foliage to decorate the houses, stacking of gigantic bonfires on the highest hills of the neighbourhood, and the making of 'sun wheels' – these were wheels, covered with hemp and tow and smeared with pitch. At sunset all the inhabitants made their way to the hilltop. The master of ceremonies lit the fire, as the crowd cheered, shouted and danced around in jubilation; these revels continued until midnight. Mothers passed their young children across the flames as a protection against witchcraft, while the youths and young men jumped over the fire and danced round it:

In the meantime the 'sun wheel' covered with its inflammable materials was pushed to the top of the hill, and at a given signal was set on fire and sent spinning down the hill to symbolise the beginning of the sun's declension. This feature of the festivities was common in this district, Wyrley, near Walsall, being one of the last places in England where it was observed. Here, as the

wheel was started on its descent, the people all shouted the
following mystic rhyme:

> Push the wheel up Worley bonk,
>   Comin' up, comin' up,
> Push the wheel down Worley bonk,
>   Goin' down, goin' down.
> Singe the tails of imp and witch,
> Burn them up in the deepest ditch,
> Uh! Uh! Uh!

This was an allusion to the popular tradition that on Midsummer
Eve the witches and evil spirits infested the air, and worked their
malice on the people. Hence the latter not only built bonfires as
a protection, being a purifier and destroyer of infection, but they
also gathered fern seed in a white handkerchief, and carried it in
their pockets to render them invisible against witches, and set the
church bells ringing at intervals from mid-day to midnight.

The young people danced round the fires, until they had all but
burned out, around midnight. On the way home the older folk
sometimes carried burning torches from the fire, to give them further
protection from evil spirits. When they reached their houses they
would sit and chat, until the torches had burned out or until the
night watchman made his round and told them to go to bed or be
brought before the justices for disturbing the peace. On this special
night additional watchmen were appointed to keep a check on the
empty houses in case of attempted burglary and to make sure the
revellers were safe as they moved between home and hillside. It is not
unusual to find entries in the church registers relating to the
watchmen; for example, this in the registers of St Leonard's Church,
Bilston:

	s.	d.	
1689—Paid for three loads of coal			
for the Watch at Midsummer.	1	6	(7½p)

In the middle ages it was the custom for Staffordshire farmers to
'perambulate the cornfields', on Midsummer Eve. They carried
lighted torches intended to protect the crops against mildew and

blight; few would risk going to bed before the circuit was completed. The people placed straws crosswise at every entrance to the village, and at the thresholds of their homes, to protect them against witches. On the lintels of their doors there were horseshoes, to keep out all foul and mischievous spirits:

> That fly or crawl, or run,
> Between the rising and the setting sun
> Ere the midsummer eve be done.

Midsummer Eve was a powerful time for witches and evil spirits, hence the number and variety of protections against evil. But it was also a time when young girls could find out what kind of a husband they were likely to get. If they plucked a daisy and chanted 'Rich man, beggar man, poor man, thief, tell me daisy, who shall be chief', as they plucked off the petals, one by one, the secret would be revealed. This charm is still popular today, though it is applied generally at any time of the year, and the items counted might be prune or cherry-stones rather than daisy-petals.

July

The only notable event in this month was the Wolverhampton Wool Fair and Procession which fell into disrepute during the late eighteenth century, after its original purpose had been virtually usurped by a pleasure fair. It had been founded in the reign of Edward III, when Wolverhampton was granted the right to hold an annual wool fair for the Midlands:

> This privilege was granted in the year 1354, when the staple of wool was removed from Flanders to England, and established in sundry places in this country, ... Wolverhampton soon became a busy mart for the sale of wool, and merchants from all parts, not only of England, but the Continent, came here to make their purchases or dispose of their skins.

The fair turned Wolverhampton from a sleepy farming town of a few hundred people into a busy, bustling market town, catering for a large portion of the country's wool trade and playing host to traders from all nations, as well as supporting and developing considerable related trades such as tanning, wool-combing and fell-mongering (trading in skins). Wolverhampton also held extensive celebrations to mark tribute to St Blaise, the patron saint of wool-combers; these celebrations took place during the time the wool fair was in existence.

It began on 9 July, but proclamations concerning the opening of the staple were made on the three days preceding the fair by the town-crier, who stood on the High Green (now Queen Square) at twelve noon to make his official announcements. The 'rows', where the wool was sold, were made up, the houses for the visitors were chosen, and limits of the mart established; within these limits, all transactions had to take place. On the morning of the fair the Mayor, bailiffs, constables, merchants, burghers and foreigners attended early service. Then the procession for 'walking' the fair was formed:

First of all came the proprietors of the burgage-houses on horseback, headed by the constables; then came the Mayor, sheriff, and bailiffs of the staple, attended by the crier, whose duty it was when the procession reached the mart to proclaim with loud voice. 'That the staple was open for ye lawful transaction of business according to ye laws and customs of ye towne.' To these succeeded the dean and chapter in their ecclesiastical vestments, ... Then came the sheepshearers, fellmongers, weighers, packers, and tanners, bearing a huge bale of wool to illustrate the character of the merchandise they were about to sell. To these succeeded the men in armour, indicating that it was to them the merchandise was entrusted to guard against theft. Then followed the musicians playing upon harp, rebec, psalterium, and such other instruments of music as were available, ...

Behind the musicians marched the merchants from England and the continent, who had come to trade, and finally the men, women and children of the district, who had come for a day out at the fair. The procession made its way to the High Green, where the town-crier made proclamation of the fair, and read out the various business laws relating to it. Next, the Mayor and his party of bailiffs, burgage owners, invited merchants and other guests, made their way to the town house, to have a meal. Officially the fair lasted for eight days, but it is said to have continued for as long as two weeks. During this time the men-at-arms patrolled the streets of the town, maintaining law and order. At the conclusion of the fair, the town-crier made the circuit of the staple, calling upon everyone to retire peacefully to rest under protection of 'God and the Mayor'. This last night was generally spent in music, dancing, drinking and singing.

By the end of the eighteenth century, the fair had fallen into disrepute. In 1789 'walking the fair' was omitted for the first time and the rowdy, unlawful mobs that attended kept the ordinary folk away. Over the years leading up to the end of the 18th century fewer and fewer bona fide traders attended, and eventually it became a pleasure fair that also supported a variety of itinerant vendors of beads and baubles, quite unrelated to the original traders in wool.

August

Like July, August was a sparse month for customs and traditions but it featured a most important and unusual custom, the Tutbury Court of Minstrels and the bull-running.

Tutbury Castle, home of John of Gaunt, the Duke of Lancaster, became a centre of musical activity in the mid-fourteenth century; musicians crowded there from all parts of the land to take part in the festivities arranged for visitors. Inevitably there was argument and disagreement among the minstrels and John of Gaunt found it necessary to adopt some means of keeping the peace and arbitrating between them. In 1374 he had married a Spanish princess and brought her back to Tutbury; by 1377 he had established his Tutbury Court of King's Minstrels and the Bull Running. He appointed a King of the Minstrels, who had various officers under him. They were empowered to apprehend and arrest any minstrels breaking the laws of the Charter or refusing to carry out their services to the Honor of Tutbury. The Charter was granted to the King of the Minstrels on 22 August in the fourth year of the reign of Richard II. The original Charter was written in Norman French and entitled Carta le Roy de Minstralx and was translated by Robert Plot:

JOHN By the Grace of God King of Castile and Leon, Duke of Lancaster, to all them who shall see or hear these our Letters greeting. Know ye we have ordained constituted and assigned to our well-beloved King of the Minstrells in our Honor of Tutbury, who is, or for the time shall be, to apprehend and arrest all the Minstrells in our said Honor and Franchise, that refuse to doe the Services and Minstrelsy as appertain to them to doe from ancient times at Tutbury aforesaid, yearly on the days of the Assumption of our Lady: giving and granting to the said King of the Minstrells for the time being, full power and commandement to make them reasonably to justify, and to constrain them to doe their services, and Minstrelsies, in manner as belongeth to them and as it hath been there, and of ancient times accustomed.

In due course it was found necessary to set up a special Court to deal with the various problems that arose. The Court was fixed for the day following the Feast of the Assumption of the Virgin Mary, which fell on 15 August; the minstrels also changed their day of service to this date, and received a bull for the bull-running from the Earl of Devon. Previously the bull was given by the Prior of Tutbury to:

.... the Minstrells who come to Matins there on the feast of the Assumption of the blessed Virgin, shall have a Bull given them by the Prior of Tutbury, if they can take him on this side of the River Dove which is next Tutbury; or else the Prior shall give them xld. for the enjoyment of which custom they shall give to the Lord at the said feast, yearly xxdg.

All the minstrels within the Honor, i.e. within the counties of Staffordshire, Derbyshire, Nottinghamshire, Leicestershire and Warwickshire, were obliged on pain of being fined, to congregate outside the house of the bailiff of the Honor, where they were met by the Steward of the Court or his deputy. The procession, headed by musicians, walked in twos to the parish church. The last King of the Minstrels marched immediately behind the musicians, flanked by the steward and the bailiff, or their deputies; then came the four stewards of the King of the Minstrels, each carrying a white wand. The rest of the company then followed in order. The minstrels attended the church service, for which they each paid one penny; then the company made its way to the Castle Hall or Court where, following the official opening, the various plaints and pleas were entered. The Musicians Court Roll was called and two juries were appointed; a jury of twelve men for Staffordshire and a further jury of twelve men for the other counties. The steward then gave an address in which he reminded the Court of Minstrels of their importance, and ended by asking them to proceed with the appointment of the officers for the following year:

> ... the Jurors proceed to the Election of the said Officers, the King to be chosen out of the 4 Stewards of the preceeding year, and one year out of Staffordshire, and the other out of Darbyshire interchangeably: and the 4 Stewards two of them out of Staffordshire, and two out of Darbyshire; 3 being chosen by the Jurors, and the 4th by him that keeps the Court, and the deputy Steward or Clerk.

The two juries leave the Court to make their decisions and, while they are gone, the rest of the company take part in a banquet. Upon the juries' return the new officers are appointed: the old King hands the new a white wand and then drinks his health in wine, and the retiring stewards do likewise. The new officers were then able to levy the fines inflicted by the juries of the day, one part of which went to the 'Kings Majesty' and the other for the use of the stewards. Once this part of the proceedings had been completed, all the company attended a dinner in their honour.

After the dinner the minstrels gathered at a barn, previously at the Abbey gate, where they received the bull:

> which Bull, as soon as his horns are cut off, his Ears cropt, his taile cut by the stumple, all his body smeared over with Soap, and his nose blown full of beaten pepper; in short, being made as mad as 'tis possible for him to be; after Solemn Proclamation made by the Steward, that all manner of person give way to the Bull, none being to come near him by 40 foot, any way to hinder the Minstrells, but to attend his or their safeties, every one at his perill: He is then forthwith turned out to them (anciently by the Prior) now by the Lord Devonshire or his deputy, to be taken by them and none other, within the County of Stafford between the

time of his being turned out to them, and the setting of the Sun the same day.

If the bull managed to escape into Derbyshire, he remained the property of the Duke of Devonshire. But if any of the minstrels managed to cut away a piece of the bull's hair while he was still in Staffordshire, he carried the hair to the market-cross to prove his case. Whereupon the bull was brought to the bailiff's house, collared, roped and taken to the Bull Ring in the High street, where he was baited with dogs: 'The first course being allotted for the King; the second for the Honor of the Towne; and the third for the King of the Minstrells.'

When the baiting was over, the minstrels could take the bull and do as they wished with it. Sell it or kill it and divide the meat, as they thought fit.

By the time Robert Plot had written the above account in 1686, the minstrels were 'assisted by the promiscuous multitude, that flock hither in great numbers' and the whole proceeding had acquired something of a Bank Holiday atmosphere. A hundred years later the Bull running had fallen into disrepute and, in spite of petitions from the minstrels, was finally abolished in 1778. The Tutbury Court of Minstrels also ceased to function in full, although an attenuated version took place annually in the Steward's House for some time after this date.

Robin Hood, according to one of the popular ballads, entitled *A New ballad of bold Robin Hood, shewing his birth, breeding, valour, and marriage at Titbury Bull-Running,* once attended the Tutbury Bull-running where, as the ballad title states, he was married. Earlier Robin Hood had met Clorinda, the Queen of the shepherds, and had fallen in love with her. He offered marriage on the spot but she replied:

> ... It may not be so, gentle sir,
> For I must be at Titbury feast;
> And if Robin Hood will go thither with me,
> I'll make him the most welcome guest.

The next day they made their way to Tutbury, carrying with them a buck as an offering. They were waylaid by eight ruffians who wanted the buck. Little John and Robin cut five down with their swords, the remaining three suing for quarter. Quarter granted the party continued on to Tutbury, where they enjoined the bull-baiting and called on a parson to wed Robin and Clorinda.

A more recently abandoned August custom was the ceremonial dancing that accompanied the August Bank holiday. The dance was held at various places including Betley, Chasetown, Kinver, Lapley, Lichfield, Rocester, Seighford, Silverdale, Stafford, Stretton, Walsall, Wednesbury and Wolverhampton. Most of them disappeared in the late nineteenth century, though Wolverhampton lost its dance in 1652, and Walsall as early as 1498. At Betley the dance was still performed between 1906 and 1910. The dancers, indeterminate in numbers, performed in procession, executing the figures as they moved along. They carried sticks or other substances – rope, cotton, cork – which were bound spirally with ribbons. The ribbons might hang from one or both ends of the stick and were used in dances where they were not struck together. The costume consisted of flowered hats, white shirts sewn with ribbons in a uniform arrangement, and breeches. Originally the dancers wore clogs, but these were replaced with ordinary shoes. Each carried two of the ribboned sticks or slings, and were led by a similarly dressed dancer, who controlled the others by means of a whistle and/or hand-signals. In the last years of the dance, the performers were accompanied by a black-faced 'female' with a broom, who was usually associated with rush-bearing. The dance was also performed at other times of the year.

September

September is a busy month in Staffordshire. One of the important events, certainly the best known, is the Abbots Bromley Horn Dance. It takes place annually, on the Monday after the first Sunday following 4 September. There are eleven performers in all: six dancers dressed in green jackets, breeches and green stockings—three wear white-painted reindeer horns, the other three black horns; there are three more characters, the Fool, the Hobby-horse, and the Maid Marion; finally there is the cross-bow bearer, often a small boy; one supporting musician, a melodeon player, completes the group.

The dance procession starts on the vicarage lawn at 8.30 am, and between 8.30 am and 9.00 am the dancers perform on the lawn and at the market place. At twelve noon they appear at Blithefield Hall, and from 4.30 pm on they re-appear in the market place. The dance or 'running' has two clearly defined parts, described by Douglas Kennedy:

One is the winding single file, which snakes its way forward, making ground gradually, as the Hornbearers thread what looks like a figure eight knot, tied without mixing the blacks with the whites. The second is a stationary dance in a set formed by the chain winding into a wide circle, then flattening out to make two files facing, and bringing the three white horns opposite the three black, while the Fool and Hobby face Marion and Cross-bow. The two lines advance and retire and cross sides, the 'stags' lurching head on at one another, as if butting. When the meet and cross brings the dancers back to their own side, the leading stag turns away, and followed in the usual order, he leads the little company looping and ducking on to the next stand. In their cross-country marathon from farm to farm, they occasionally stop dancing, and just walk informally at ease, chatting until the leader decides to resume making the medicine.

The 'usual order' for the company was the horn-bearers, followed by the Fool, the Hobby-horse and Maid Marion; the cross-bow brought up the rear. While the white horns have remained unchanged over the years, the other set have been variously red, blue and black. The origin of the horns is not known. They were ancient in Robert Plot's time in the mid-seventeenth century, but they are known to be tame reindeer horns, and it seems likely that the deer were indigenous. The horns are described as follows:

No. 1 $16\frac{1}{2}$lb. 31″ from tip to top, painted white
No. 2 19lb. 29″ from tip to top, painted white
No. 3 $16\frac{1}{4}$lb. 35″ from tip to top, painted brown/black
No. 4 $23\frac{1}{4}$lb. 33″ from tip to top, painted brown/black
No. 5 20lb. 38″ from tip to top, painted brown/black
No. 6 $25\frac{1}{4}$lb. 39″ from tip to top, painted white

The weights include head iron fittings and stale; the iron is hand-wrought and old, and the woodwork is sixteenth century at the latest. All the horns have several coats of paint—blue, red and cream beneath the existing colours.

The Horn Dance is a unique ritual dance of obscure origins, though many explanations of it have been put forward. Between the suggestion that it is the remnant of a church pageant, whose aim was to raise funds, and the belief that it stems from nature and fertility ritual among the Druids, lie a number of explanations. Many people thought that witchcraft was the motivating force. The wearing of stag horns was regarded as an evil practice and St. Theodore, Archbishop of Canterbury 668 - 90, in the *Liber Penitentialis,* prohibits 'any at the Kalends dressing up in the skins of herd animals or going about as a stag, or putting on the head or horns of beasts. For those who in such wise transform themselves, the penance is 3 years, for this is devilish' (Summers, *History of Witchcraft and Demonology*). Elsewhere it has been suggested that the dance is connected with the granting of forest rights to the villagers of Abbots Bromley. In a document of 1125, in the Cartularly of Abbots Bromley, the forest rights of the Abbey's local lands were bestowed upon the men of Abbots Bromley. Supposition connected with magical ritual has led to the idea that in pagan times the dance was intended as an enticement to the deer. In the same vein it was suggested that the horns were a kind of talisman, worn by primitive man to face deer with the potency of their own weapons and, after the hunt, as a sign of prowess.

At the present time the custom flourishes and the dance attracts large crowds to the village. Both factually and photographically it has become an exceptionally well-documented custom.

Another flourishing calendar custom, the Sheriff's Ride, takes place at nearby Lichfield on 8 September, the Nativity of the Blessed Virgin Mary. The Sheriff's Ride dates from a Royal Charter of 1553 which granted Lichfield county status and provided for the election of a Sheriff. Traditionally the Ride took place on 8 September but it is now held on the Saturday nearest that date. It takes the form of a perambulation of the twenty-four miles of the City boundaries, which were once marked with wood and metal stakes, and it is traditional for the Sheriff to ride on horseback, though present-day custom allows use of a car. While most perambulations take place during Rogation-tide, Lichfield is by no means unique in the county for out-of-season perambulation. Alrewas held one on 1 October in 1794 and Newcastle in March 1887, for example.

At present the Sheriff's party, who travel by horse, meet in the Market Square at 10.30 am, and from there they ride to the Guild Hall, where they join the rest of the group. The perambulation of the boundaries is begun at 11.00 am, when all the vehicles and horses set out on the journey. Various stops are made at farms and public houses to drink a stirrup cup, but the first major stop is at Freeford Manor, or Aldershaw Hall, if that is not available, where the party takes lunch between 1.00 pm and 2.00 pm. At this stop a series of horse races are held. Only those horses accompanying the Ride from the Market Square are allowed to enter, culminating in the major race for the Sheriff's Plate. The afternoon sees the continuation of the Perambulation with stirrup cups at various farms, the Horse and Jockey Inn, and the Trent Valley Hotel. When the circuit is complete, the party returns to the Guild Hall and then disperses.

Starting times and routes tend to vary, so those wishing to see the Ride should check with the Town Hall before-hand.

Wake time was an important occasion for most Staffordshire towns until well into the nineteenth century. In the north of the county Newcastle held its wake, St Giles Fair, throughout the Middle Ages. In 1590 a written charter confirmed the fair for the first Monday after St Giles Day on 1 September, but in 1753 the Borough Council changed the date to the first Monday after 11 September. The fair flourished throughout the nineteenth and early twentieth century and, though it is no longer celebrated, the 'Council Year Books' continued to list the first Monday after 11 September as Wakes Fair Day as recently as 1951. In 1901 the fair was described by a reporter for the Newcastle Guardian:

Castle Wakes are on, and the High Street is crowded with booths and roundabouts. Today and on Monday you will have to fight your way along the principal thoroughfare of the town through masses of people, bent chiefly on pleasure, and through a labyrinth of caravans, stalls, shooting galleries and flying cockerels, and avoid the blare of steam organs more powerful than harmonions, and the piercing shriek of ear-splitting sirens .... Since the trams have commenced running a great many more people than formerly are brought to the town at the Wakes.

The song Newcastle Wakes was written in 1841 and gives a good idea of the wake of that period:

Newcastle Wakes

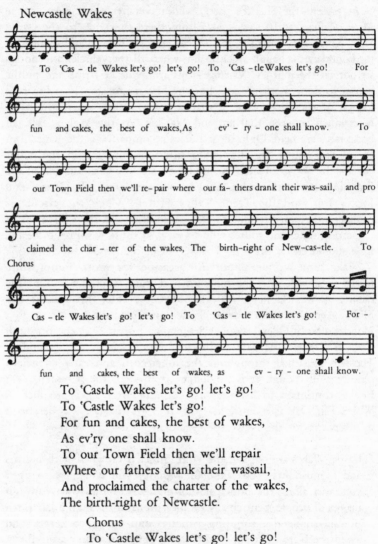

To 'Castle Wakes let's go! let's go!
To 'Castle Wakes let's go!
For fun and cakes, the best of wakes,
As ev'ry one shall know.
To our Town Field then we'll repair
Where our fathers drank their wassail,
And proclaimed the charter of the wakes,
The birth-right of Newcastle.

> Chorus
> To 'Castle Wakes let's go! let's go!
> To 'Castle Wakes let's go!
> For fun and cakes, the best of wakes,
> As ev'ry one shall know.

The sports so gay will soon repay
The enraptured anxious gazer,
Whilst wives and sweethearts on your knee
Will doubly add to pleasure.
Strike up, strike up, thou glorious band,
Fifes, fiddles, pipes and organ,
Our leader with famed Hullah's wand
Will keep time with old Morgan.

A chosen band of loyal men
That faced the rebel wars
Will stand at ease and tip the cat,
And play at prison bars.
The Italian ballad singers feast,
The chorus loud to bawl,
Whilst Billy Punky and the rest
Eat stir-pudding with an awl.

The steeple chase, the barrow race,
In bags with many a faw,
Whilst some you'll see on bended knee
Knuckeing down to taw,
And men so sage will mount the stage
In hopes to win the dollar;
With many a tug their ugly mug
Keeps grinning through the collar.

With drums and fifes and banners bright,
And men of all profession,
And champions gay in fine array,
To join in the procession.
And whilst we sing each year shall bring
Our festival so gay,
With ale and cakes our merry wakes
Upon St Matthew's Day.

Hullah's wand refers to the baton of John Hullah, 1812-84, a
well-known composer, music-teacher and conductor. The rebel wars
perhaps means the Chartist unrest; 'in bags' is the sack race; 'faw' is

fall; 'knuckeing down to taw' is a game of marbles. St Matthew's Day is 21 September. This date seems at variance with the official day, the first Monday after 11 September, though wake dates were subject to some change.

Originally the wakes were Watch Services on the Eve of the Feast of Dedication, when people left their homes at night and walked to the local church carrying lighted candles, in order to make their devotions and keep watch over the dead. The wakes were instituted in honour of the saint to whom the church was dedicated, and they were held in the churchyard. The observance gradually deteriorated, until the wake was transformed into an entertainment and the church grounds became the setting for picnics, sideshows, sports and other non-religious festivities. In the reign of Henry VIII and Elizabeth strenuous efforts were made to control wake proceedings and, after the Reformation, the wakes were banished to the market-places.

During the nineteenth century the approach of wake time found Staffordshire folk cleaning, repairing and painting their homes in readiness for wake visitors. It was customary to keep open house on Wake Sunday and Monday and, those who could afford it, provided a special wake brew and wake joint. Apart from the sports and pastimes mentioned in the Newcastle Wake songs, it was usual to have cock-fighting, bull-baiting, bear-baiting, dog-fighting, and other blood sports as part of the wake festivities, in the early part of the 19th century and before.

Other towns that held their wakes in September included Stone, in the north, and Brierley Hill, in the far south of the county; both wakes fell on 29 September, the Feast of St Michael and All Angels. The importance of the wakes might be gathered from the words of an old Gornal woman of the nineteenth century, who said the four seasons were 'Chrissmus and Aystertite, Our Waake and Whissuntite'.

Newcastle-under-Lyme was also the scene of a Mock Mayor ceremony which, prior to the passing of the Municipal Reform Act in 1835, had taken place for two hundred years. As soon as the official Mayor-making ceremony was completed, the freemen gathered at the Market Cross and chose a Mock Mayor; the form of the ceremony followed that of the official one, with suitable changes to amuse the crowd that gathered to watch. Newcastle was granted a Charter of Incorporation by Queen Elizabeth in 1590 which, among other considerations, confirmed the right of the 'Burgesses' to elect a Mayor. The privilege was later usurped by the members of the Corporation, thus depriving the Burgesses of their Charter rights. In order to demonstrate their disapproval and to show some measure of claiming the right, they devised the Mock Mayor election. Joseph Mayer, writing in *Proceedings of the Historical Society of Lancashire and Cheshire,* 1850-51, describes the ceremony fully:

His Mock Worship was, with all the gravity befitting such an occasion, summoned, by the shrill sound of a Nany-goat's horn, to appear before his brother-townsmen and show cause why—always provided if—he had any objection to that most-devoutedly-to-be-desired and that most glorious and honourable elevation to the state of Mayor of the Borough, with all the customary priviledges of getting drunk, and fining himself publicly as an example, &c. Then, with great stateliness of step, and severe magisterial countenance some well-beloved fellow-townsman was conducted to the top step, and there invested with those most becoming and costly robes of state, and that magic wand of office, so capable of doing justice, on the person whose head it knocked.

The 'Mayor' then introduces his wife to the gathering and:

His Worship having commanded silence to be observed, the Town-crier, with the usual preliminaries of bell-ringing, &c. read the following proclamation:
'O Yes! O Yes! O Yes!' This is to give Notice, First, that, by the advice of my Beadle, Mace-bearers and Bum-bailiffs, I do hereby declare and proclaim that it shall be lawful for any man or set of men to put their hands into their breeches pockets – if there be their purses – and give and pay over to our exchequer any sum less than one hundred guineas, that shall deem to him or them fit, in order that we may drink his or their jolly good health in a quart of ale a-piece, for which we, as well on our part as on yours, promise him or them the distinguished honour of three huzzas, and may they live to do the like again next year.
Secondly, – That we, after mature consideration, do allow any grocer – so he do it handsomely and pleasantly to his own feelings – the never-to-be-appreciated and valuable priviledge (which must

be thought a sufficient reward unto him and his children for ever) of giving unto our revenue collectors, as much tobacco as he pleases; provided always, and it is hereby declared, that the amount must not exceed one hundredweight, but shall, at the same time, be enough to serve all the old women, as well as our worthy selves.

Thirdly, – that Morgan, the pipe-maker, as his hereditary right, which we hereby acknowledge, may, if he likes, furnish us with saggar pipes to smoke the aforesaid tobacco with; in consideration whereof, we pledge our honour (here two squeaks from the Nanny-goat horn) that nobody else shall.

Fourthly, – Our worthy Mayor giveth notice, and commandeth that all canting, gin-drinking women be brought before him, that he may punish them with the Bridle, kept by him for that purpose; and he recommendeth his brother freemen to eat plenteously of roast-beef and plum-pudding, to gain which they must work more and drink less; and further, that all persons found drunk in the streets after this notice will be put in the stocks for one hour and thirteen minutes.

Fifthly, and lastly, – We do hereby say, as commanded by our beloved wife, for the benefit of all young maidens, (after painful experience on our own part), that it is better to be married than single; and in proof of our firm conviction of the same, we do thus publicly declare, sign, and seal this our proclamation with a kiss.'

A long flourish on the Nanny-goat's horn at the close of this performance, after which the procession formed, and, with her ladyship enthroned on a donkey, his Worship and the "goodlie companie" marched through the principal streets of the town, collecting the revenue for a jollification at the Market-cross in the evening.

God save the King, the Mayor, and the People.'

It seems that the ceremony caused considerable annoyance among members of the corporation, since instances of the Mock Mayor being put in the stocks have been recorded. At one time the custom was successfully banned for, in 1833, following a prolonged legal harangue, the ceremony was re-started after the Charter had been confirmed. In the same account Mayer describes the characters who took part in the election:

His Worship is arrayed in a calf-skin tunic, fastened with a skewer round the neck, a black Staffordshire bull's hide for a gown, and a sheepskin wig. In his dexter hand he holds his wand of office, and his civic chain and glass are represented by horses' manes and the prison-door key, the latter emblematical of the reign of Bailiffs.

His worship is supported on the right hand by the Town-clerk, a person of very knowing look, and quite alive to the tricks of the law, as is fully indicated by the expressive position of his left thumb. Under his other arm he holds the Charter of the Borough, which the good Burgesses, fearing parchment would not be lasting enough, have inscribed on a hide of leather. On the left side is the Bum-bailiff, *alias* Head Constable, with his truncheon, about to dislodge a sweep, who in return is about to powder his Worship's wig with his soot bag. The two figures right and left are Mace-bearers, as seen by the splendid cabbages which they carry; and the Bellman, in his Phrygian cap and shaggy skin dress, is reading the proclamation.

The description is taken from a print of the 1833 Mock Mayor ceremony; characters include the Mayor's wife on her donkey and the members of the legal Corporation. It was customary for the public-school children to 'bar-out' their teachers on the day of the ceremony, and other boys and girls claimed exemption from work. The Mock Mayor ceremony was copied by the district of Hanley and Shelton. The first nomination was made on 18 September 1783 and the following year it took place on 30 September. In Hanley and Shelton it was also known as the Venison Feast, because of the annual donation of half a buck by the Marquis of Stafford. More recently some of the citizens of Wednesbury held a Mock Mayor election when the town received its municipal charter in 1886.

The final September custom, last noted in the early nineteenth century, was called 'crying the mare'. The sport took place at harvest-time, when the reapers tied together the tops of the last blades of corn, 'which is "mare"', and then stood some distance away and threw their sickles in an attempt to cut the knot. The winner received the congratulations of his competitors and the sheaf of corn from which the Christmas dish of 'frumity' or 'frumenty' was made; this was also a wake dish, further known by the names 'furmety' and 'frumentum' at Leek. It was made from creed wheat with milk, raisins, currants, nutmegs and spices. A miniature sheaf was also plaited from a part of the corn, and this was hung from the rafters until the next harvest, and was thought to bring good luck to the household; this part of the custom is akin to the corn dolly once made by many farming households to bring good luck and to keep the 'spirit of the corn' alive until the following year.

October

October has never been a busy month in the folk calendar, although it was punctuated with one or two fairs and wakes and still ends with Hallowe'en activities. Burton on Trent once held a Hiring Fair on the Monday after Michaelmas, and Leek also held one on October 18th, which coincided with Leek Wakes. The Wakes featured all the sports and pastimes outlined for the Newcastle Wakes and the day was associated with certain traditional wake foods, such as frumenty, roast beef, boiled swedes, red cabbage, wake cakes, etc. Further south, Rugeley held an annual fair for the sale of sheep, cattle and horses; Staffordshire seems to have been something of a centre for the sale of horses with fairs at Newcastle under Lyme, Eccleshall, Wednesbury, Burton and Penkridge all claiming specialist activity in the sale of horses. Without doubt Penkridge was the chief fair for such sales, though Rugeley also became an important centre. Burton had some four annual fairs: the last was a six-day fair, starting on 24 October. Pitt says, in his *County Topography:*

> The principal lasts six days; during the first five days more fine horses, particularly of the black breed, are usually exposed to sale than at any other fair in the kingdom. The sixth day is the festival of St Modwen (29 October) and is appropriated to the sale of cheese, and to a variety of sports and pastimes.

St Modwen's Fair was granted to the Abbot of Burton by King John and Molyneux, a Burton historian in the mid-nineteenth century, claimed that the fair once lasted three days 'but now and for many years past, of nine days' duration, terminating on the day it formerly began, namely 29 October'.

Hallowe'en or All Hallows Even, on the last day of October, is the eve of All Saints Day on 1 November. Traditionally it was a time when the spirit world came alive, and when young girls, by various means, might learn the name of their husbands-to-be. However the date does not seem to have been one of celebration and entertainment on anything like the scale it is today in the County. Hallowe'en parties are now common, and they are often attended in fancy dress and masks, as are the parties for the young children, who also scoop out turnips to make the traditional Hallowe'en lanterns. The night has a certain mystique, created by the mock belief that spirits, ghosts, devils and other strange beings are likely to be found abroad.

November

November 1st, All Saints Day, and 2 November, All Souls Day, marked a continuation of the observances begun on 31 October with Hallowe'en. Throughout these two days it was customary for the poor of the parish to 'go a souling'. Parties of soul cakers would travel the district, singing the souling song at the doors of the well-to-do, for which they hoped to receive soul cakes, apples, ale, or money. The soul cakes were often baked in large numbers by housewives, in readiness for the soulers and others who might call; they were flat round cakes. The cakes were common in the north of the County, but do not seem to have been popular in the south, even though the custom of souling was widespread throughout the County. Traditionally those claiming their dole did so as a reward for praying for the souls of the dead, and at one time the 'soul' bell was rung the day long at short intervals. In her *Shropshire Folklore*, Charlotte Burne comments: 'I have been told by a middle-aged woman from Houghton, Staffordshire, on the authority of her mother, that souling parties were wont to go away shouting "a good house", or "a bad house", according to the treatment they had received.'

This would be in the mid-nineteenth century, at the time when adults still went souling, but by the end of the nineteenth century the custom had become a preserve of the children. The earlier rhymes and ditties, sung or chanted by the adults, tended to make reference to ale:

> We'll have a jug of your best October beer,
> And we'll come no more a-souling till
> This time next year.

With talking and walking we get very dry,
So I hope you good neighbours will
never us deny.
Put your hand in your pocket
And pull out your keys,
Go down into your cellar
And draw us what you please!

A similar version, intact with its tune, comes from further north than Eccleshall, the home of the first rhyme:

We are two or three hea – rty lads All in one row – And we Shall not come gui – sing Till this time next year, Put your hand in your pock – ets, Pull out your bright keys And go down to your cel – lar – Bring up what you please.

We are two or three hearty lads
All in one row,
And we shall not come guising
Till this time next year.
Put your hands in your pockets
Pull out your bright keys
And go down to your cellar
Bring up what you please.

At Leek it was customary to perform the mummers play and have the hobby horse along for the souling; elsewhere the mummers generally featured at Christmas time and the hobby, though seen at other times of the year, was not a part of souling. The traditional soul drink was known as 'lambswool' and the apples requested in many versions of the souling ditty would be used to make this drink of hot spiced ale and roasted apples. A very early and complete version of the souling song was noted down from an old Staffordshire woman in 1824:

> Soul! soul! for an apple or two;
> If you've got no apples, pears will do,
> Soul! soul! for your soul's sake,
> Pray, goodmistress, a soul cake!
> An apple or pear, a plum or a cherry,
> Or any good thing to make us merry.
> St Peter was a good old mon,
> And so for his sake give us one;
> None of your worst, but one of your best,
> So God may send your souls to rest.
> Up with your kettles, and down with your pons,
> Give us a Soul Cake, and we'll be gone!

This one was to be sung on All Saints Day, 1 November, following a special evening service for soulers, and the following day they would go about singing:

> Soul Cake Day is come and gone,
> And we again are here;
> And if you've neither apples nor pears,
> Give us a pot of beer.
> That we may dance and merrily sing,
> As far as we do go;
> And when we come to the very next house,
> We hope they'll serve us so.

The first of these two chants is very similar to that used on St Clement's Day, later in the month.

Guy Fawkes night on 5 November is still widely celebrated in Staffordshire, the main features remaining unchanged. The traditional bonfire, fireworks, burning of the Guy and roasting of potatoes and chestnuts in the bonfire are all observed.

During the nineteenth century the children made their collection for the Guy and would sing the following ditty:

Pray a ha'penny for a taper
An' a ha'penny for a match,
A ha'penny for a faggot,
An another for a match.
Pray gee us some money
For crackers and powder
To charge all our canons,
An' mack them sound louder.
Pray gee us a jacket,
To dress Guy the infernal,
As he burns in the flames
Of a fire eternal.

Another rhyme used prior to the night and on the night itself reminds folks of the nature of the Plot:

Good gentle folk pray,
Remember this day,
To which your kind notice we bring,
Here's the figure of sly
Old villanous Guy,
Who wanted to murder the King.
With powder a store
He bitterly swore,
As he skulked in the vaults to prepare
How the Parliament crew,
Should all be blown up in the air.
So please to remember
The 5th of November,
Gunpowder treason and plot,
There's the best of all reason,
Why Gunpowder Treason,
Should never be forgot.

The figure of Guy Fawkes was hoisted high onto the top of the prepared bonfire and, as it caught fire, it was bombarded with turf, rotten vegetables and other missiles. As the figure finally collapsed and burned, the gathering would sing:

Good people all, this is the day
When old Guy Faux and his plotting priests
Tried to blow up Parliament;
But they were all caught in the nick of time,
Hung high in a noose,
And to old Nick were sent;
Where they burn in a fire
That gets hotter and higher,
And roast like a Christmas goose,
Huzza! Huzza! Huzza!

At the Wolverhampton bonfire night in 1826, a procession took place with the people all dressed up in fancy disguises. They carried a dilapidated figure of Guy Fawkes in their midst, dressed as a scarecrow, and placed on a hurdle. When the procession reached High Green, now Queens Square, Guy Fawkes was placed on the fire and the boys sang the last six lines of the second bonfire verse. For this event, and in general, the bonfire night bellringers were paid from the street collections and from the churchwardens account.

The 23 November marked the Feast of St Clement and this day was set aside for Clementing, a similar custom to Souling; in general Clementing was more popular in South Staffordshire and Souling in the north. Robert Plot in his *Natural History of Staffordshire*, comments 'a pot is marked on the Clogg almanac against St. Clement's Day from the ancient custom of going about that night to beg drink to make merry with.' The Staffordshire Clogg Almanacs were in use at the time of the Saxon Conquest, and it is clear from the available evidence that the customs associated with the day are very old. In the nineteenth century the day was regarded as something of a festive occasion, especially by the children, who in many areas were allowed, or took, time off from school to go about the streets knocking on doors and singing or chanting the couplet:

An apple, a pear, a plum, or a cherry,
Or anything else to make us all merry.

This was one of the couplets used in Walsall, but most towns and villages also had longer versions that were popularly sung. In reply to a newspaper appeal for information on the Clemeny customs that

I made in 1965, Mr W. H. Hickman of Crewe wrote: 'It must be well over 70 years ago since my "loud and clear" voice performed for the Edification of the gentry for you may be sure we chose only the houses which, outwardly at least, looked as though there was likely to be a welcome response.'

Mr Hickman, who was born and lived in Wolverhampton for a good many years, describes the tune to the Clemeny verse he quotes as a see-sawing chant of no particular musical merit. In the late nineteenth century he travelled the streets with his friends, as did many children, singing a ditty similar to this one;

> Clemeny! Clemeny! Clemeny raine!
> A good red apple and a pint of wine;
> Some of your mutton and some of your veal,
> If it is good, pray give me a deal;
> If it is not, pray give me some salt.
> Butler, butler, fill your bowl;
> If thou fillest of the best,
> The Lord'll send your soul to rest;
> If they fillest it of the small,
> Down goes butler, bowl, and all.
> Pray, good mistress, send to me
> One for Peter, one for Paul,
> One for Him who made us all;
> Apple, pear, plum, or cherry,
> Any good thing to make us merry;
> A bouncing buck and a velvet chair,
> Clement comes but once a year;
> Off with the pot and on with the pan,
> A good red apple and I'll be gone.

Pan is commonly pronounced 'pon' in the Black Country. This longer version, or one very similar, was also sung by the children of Walsall, who walked the streets of the town, chanting the rhyme, prior to the distribution of apples by Corporation officials, who had a sum of money at their disposal sepcifically for this purpose. Dr Willmore, in his *History of Walsall,* recalls that:

the old custom of throwing apples and nuts from the Windows of the Guildhall on St Clement's Day was abolished in 1850. Up to this time the boys of the Grammar School were admitted to the Sessions Court, where they scrambled for the apples thrown from the Magisterial Bench by the ladies and gentlemen assembled there, while outside, in addition to the fruit, the crowd were amused with hot coppers scattered amongst them by Griffin, the Town Crier.

The occasion was also generally known as 'Bite Apple Night' after the game of Bite Apple: the fruit was suspended from a piece of string and swung from side to side. The players stood round and attempted to take a bite while holding their hands behind them. They might also be supplied with forks: the trick then was to spear the apple and take a bite before the other players. Alternatively a wooden lath was attached to the string: the apple was balanced on one end and a lighted candle on the other. The players endeavoured to bite it without being burnt by the candle.

A popular belief at Wednesbury was related to the apples used in local observances. A young girl who wished to find out the name of her future husband would pare an apple, keeping the paring in one piece. She then moved away from her companions and threw the paring over her left shoulder. The shape assumed as it lay on the floor was matched to the nearest capital letter it resembled and this was the initial of her husband-to-be.

St Clement was adopted by the blacksmiths as their patron saint. His legend describes how he was martyred: the saint was tied to an anchor and drowned in the sea. The water then retreated for seven days every year until his body was visible, still attached to the anchor and resting in a marble tomb. The blacksmiths were evidently attracted to Clement because he was martyred with a metal anchor, and it seems likely that his popularity in South Staffordshire, an area predominantly concerned with the manufacture of metal goods, arose from the same reason.

December

Doleing, mumping and gooding were three of the names given to the customs that surrounded St Thomas's Day in Staffordshire. It fell on 21 December and was commonly used for the distribution of

church doles, often called St Thomas's Dole. The custom was similar
to those associated with All Saints Day and St Clement's Day, when
the poor of the parish would visit the homes of the well-to-do,
begging a handout of cash or food. Local historian Lawley recalls
that:

> In the days of the Georges, when red cloaks were commonly worn
> by the beldames of every parish, it was a usual sight to see, in the
> grey light of a December morning, groups of figures, bent and
> withered, going from door to door, wrapped in these curious
> garments, and hear them piping, 'in a childish treble voice', the
> following rhyme:
>
> > Well a day, well a day,
> > St Thomas goes too soon away,
> > Then your gooding we do pray,
> > For the good times will not stay,
> > St Thomas grey, St Thomas grey,
> > The longest night and the shortest day,
> > Please to remember St Thomas's Day.

The poor also made extensive use of the public doles given by the
church and, in some places, by the civil authority. The doles were
often legacies left by the well-to-do in the hands of the clergy or the
churchwardens, whose instructions were to distribute the money to
the poor and needy on the Sunday nearest to St Thomas's Day; most
of the 19th-century writers point out that giving doles on the 21st
ensured that everyone would have food and warm clothing for the
Christmas festival. At Wednesbury and Darlaston the dole included
the giving of overcoats, woollen gowns, blankets, fuel, and other
basic requirements; at Burton on Trent two charities were held on
St Thomas's Day. One was known as 'widows Groats'; the other was
a distribution of the rents obtained from a benefaction property by
two Town's Masters, who were once the retiring Parish Constables
and later the retiring churchwardens. At Cheadle those who made
private donations to the poor were generally handed a sprig of
mistletoe, a plant held in high esteem, as we shall see.

The majority of December customs and traditions revolved round
Christmas. The special foods, carol-singing, performance of mum-

ming plays, giving of presents, decoration of church and home, all centred on the celebration of the birth of Christ and many of those customs and traditions still survive.

Food seems to have had pride of place at Christmas time and few changes have occurred in this respect. Even the poor families of late 19th century England could be certain of some of the special Christmas foods, since the well-off saw the occasion as one for giving and sharing. Those who could afford a full board would have a variety of meats – boar's head, brawn, capons, game, beef, mutton and pork, which were cooked in exotic spices and washed down with the special Christmas ales and wines. The main course would be followd by plum pudding, mince pies and other sweets, which were also helped on their way with beer and wine.

On Christmas Eve 'toast and swig' was a traditional north Staffordshire supper. It consisted of spiced ale, taken with small pieces of toasted cheese. But the main feasting started on Christmas morning, when folks in many parts of the County ate a pre-lunch dish of furmety, which we have described in the September custom of 'Crying the Mare'. Furmety was made from the actual miniature wheat-sheaf that had been hung from the rafters at harvest-time, when the young men and women went 'a-leasing', specifically to gather up the gleanings. In certain parishes, those who could not afford a proper Christmas dinner could go along to the vicar's house, where they would, by tradition, receive a Christmas dinner. This custom took place in Aldridge but a payment of 6d was substituted eventually, with which the vicar exhorted each of his parishioners to 'regale his family at home'.

At Stafford the Chamberlain of the Corporation made a payment of 6s. with which a quantity of plums was purchased to be distributed 'among the inhabitants of certain old houses in the liberty of Forebridge'. The custom is said to arise from the kindness of some individual who, hearing some children complaining about not having any plums for the Christmas pudding, counted the houses in the district and made arrangements for the supply of a pound of plums per household. During the observance of the custom, the plums were purchased with the 6s., divided into equal parcels and delivered to the households, irrespective of the circumstances of the householders; the tradition appears to have died out in the mid-nineteenth century.

A universal drink for Christmas Eve, Christmas Day and Boxing Day was 'lambswool' which was also drunk on other occasions such as Clemeny in November. The drink, a concoction of roasted apples in strong ale, which was spiced and sugared, was commonly given to work-people by managers and small employers in South Staffordshire. It was made in large glazed earthenware vessels, known in the Black Country as 'a jowl', and ladled round the company until empty, when the drinkers sang a carol.

Another popular Christmas drink was the wine made from elder berry. The elder tree was regarded as a very significant plant and Robert Plot, in his *Natural History of Staffordshire*, comments:

> The superstitious veneration that some people in this county, especially in the moorlands, amongst the ancienter sort, and sometimes those of very good fashion, owe to the Fraximus Sylvestris (or Quicken) tree – which they firmly believe preserves them from the fascination of evil spirits, upon which account many are very careful to have a walking stick of it, and stick boughs of it about their beds.

If only the 'ancienter sort' still clung to the belief in North Staffordshire in the seventeenth century, it still had general currency in the Black Country, South Staffordshire, in the nineteenth century. A number of local journalists and writers comment on the custom of making wine from the elder berries, which was kept until Christmas and drunk as mulled wine, in honour of the general protection afforded by the tree at Christmas against 'the mischievous powers of witches and demons'.

Two other widely held beliefs connected with food and drink were that bread baked on Christmas Eve would never grow mouldy, and that to eat mince pies before Christmas Eve brought bad luck; although those who abstained until then would have as many happy months in the following year as the number of houses in which they ate mince pies between Christmas and Twelfth Night. The Christmas season was marked by a number of other beliefs. Mistletoe, like elder, had protective qualities against evil, and anyone who placed a little mistletoe in a small bag and hung it round their neck was safe from any malevolent witches and evil spirits. At Bilston, and elsewhere, it was not uncommon for the inhabitants, in the early 19th century, to draw chalk lines across the streets and lanes at the edge of the town. A cross was made at the end of each line and, by this means, witch, warlock, goblin and elf were prevented from entering. As a further protection, particularly for those without mistletoe or elder, two straws could be placed crossways on the lintel of the door; the straws would be put in position on Christmas Eve. On a lighter note, the north Staffordshire folk believed that if the sun shone through the apple trees at noon on Christmas Day, a good crop could be expected in the following season.

The custom of decorating homes and churches with holly, ivy, laurel, mistletoe etc. has always been widespread and it is still common practice today. People still hold to the custom of leaving decorations and cards until Twelfth Day before taking them down. At the turn of the century many removed the decorations on Candlemas Day, 2 February, when they would be burnt; it is also recorded that, in the mid-nineteenth century, the Christmas decorations used at Stone Mill were taken to the cowsheds and fed to the cattle to prevent them 'casting' their calves.

Mistletoe was a much-used plant and most Staffordshire homes still hang up a sprig or two in door- or hall-ways; the custom of kissing beneath the mistletoe is carried on. The plant was believed to have medicinal powers and at one time it was customary to place mistletoes on the altar of St Peter's church, Wolverhampton, to be blessed by the priests, then divided and given to the congregation, who used it as a 'cure-all', though it was regarded as particularly effective in treating fevers; none of the local accounts say how the 'medicine' was taken. Belief in its curative powers was still widespread in the early twentieth century. Mistletoe as a safeguard against witchcraft has already been mentioned, but it also gave rise to other beliefs. Lawley tells us that: 'It is considered unlucky to take down mistletoe that is hung up at Christmas time until the Christmas Eve following; and in some houses the old mistletoe bush is still to be seen hanging from the ceiling, dry and dusty, but sacred until its purpose is served.'

The practice of the church bells 'ringing-in' Christmas morning at twelve midnight is no longer continued, though many families gather to welcome in Christmas day, much as they do for the New Year; the larger party gatherings for Christmas Eve are also popular, though the original purpose behind the parties, to celebrate the birth of Christ, is not foremost in the evening. In the early-to-mid-nine-teenth century the family gathering was seldom dispensed with as Lawley tells us:

Another custom, once common in the district, was that of sitting up on Christmas Eve till twelve o'clock to welcome the birthday of the Saviour with a carol – in which all the family and servants joined – and in wishing each other a 'Merry Christmas' over a bowl of wine. No family ever retired to bed until this ceremony was over, even though they were certain that the waits would serenade them from the streets as soon as the clock struck.

Traditionally the waits did not start their music until twelve midnight on Christmas Eve. When the hour struck, the bands of musicians playing seasonable tunes would begin their tour of the town. Some played only instrumental music; others performed on instruments and sang carols, while in the industrial Black Country the Brass Bands and Salvation Army bands also took part as waits. In some parts of the county the waits were about long before Christmas Eve, as Plant in his *History of Cheadle* says:

Whether the mummery of 'guisers' who wait about the parish at Christmas when I was a boy do still, I do not know. The church singers and ringers went about the parish making collections for their services. Christmas Waits or musicians, who for a month previously had gone about the parish giving night serenades, on Christmas Day and following days, called on the parishioners with their music and made collections.

In the Black Country a 'relic of the timbril waits' is described in detail by Lawley in his *Staffordshire Customs:*

For several weeks before each Christmas, groups of boys were in the habit of starting early in the morning through the streets carrying old tin kettles or saucepans, upon which they beat vehemently in order to extract as much noise as possible, so as to wake up the colliers and ironworkers. These noisy 'waits' started soon after five, and, so far as we can surmise, seem to have commenced their perambulations soon after 1775, about which

time the residents of Wolverhampton, in vestry assembled, decided
that there should in future be no money paid to the bell keeper
for ringing curfew. Whether the 'tin-kettlers' were paid for
making their noisy music or not, we are unable to say, but that
the practice was kept up in the depth of winter seems to suggest
that it was kept up by some payment, as a substitute for the
"curfew", especially as the boys were not molested by the anceint
watchman. This is no doubt a survival of the ancient "timbril
waits", once common throughout England.

Christmas Eve was also said to be a busy time for the farm
animals, since at twelve midnight the ox, ass, cow and horse all fell
on their knees worshipping, in recognition of the birth of Jesus
Christ in a manger. Another widespread tale that relates to Christmas
Eve concerns a spot near Wednesfield, where a Saxon noble attempted to build a church to mark his conversion to the Christian
faith. The spot happened to be inhabited by fairies who, resenting
the intrusion, carried off all the stones laid during the daytime under
cover of darkness. They were so persistent that the nobleman
eventually gave up the attempt, but, it is said that, on Christmas Eve,
when fairies and the like have no power, the underground ringing
of bells could be heard on the spot, and some claimed to have heard
a heavenly choir singing *Gloria in Excelsis*. The same tale is found in
other counties.

Christmas Eve was once the occasion for an elaborate sword dance
which Lawley saw in his youth and described in detail:

Another custom no longer celebrated, was what was once known
as the 'sword dance'. It was performed on Christmas Eve, before
the residence of the principal inhabitants, by bands of colliers,
sometimes as many as twenty in a band, decorated with sprigs of
holly and mistletoe, and armed with wooden swords. Two of their
number, called Tommy and Bessy, were usually dressed in skins
and masks of the most grotesque fashions, making them look not
unlike some of the fantastic figures in the Saxon mummeries.
They were accompanied by a fiddler or musician of some kind, and
two or three lads, also fantastically dressed, carrying lanterns made
of immense swedes, hollowed out and cut to represent grim
human faces, to give the group as grotesque an appearance as

possible. They proceeded at first slowly to cross their wooden swords, changing their position to the music of a fiddle. While the dance was proceeding the speed of their movements was gradually increased until they seemed to be engaged in mortal combat. Their proceedings were accompanied by the singing of a carol, which they timed to end with the dance. Tommy and Bessy meanwhile went through a dance on their own account, putting themselves into a variety of ridiculous postures to rouse the mirth and liberality of the spectators. The carol, sung on this occasion, the present writer took down at the time, and it ran as follows:

> Christmas comes but once a year,
> Give us of your beef and beer,
> If the beer is getting low,
> And the beef is gone also,
> Wine and mince pies give instead
> Or money that we may be fed;
> Merry is the Christmas time
> Merry is our simple rhyme,
> A 'Merry Christmas' to you all,
> And so to end it, that is all.

The sword dance described by Lawley seems to be a combination of mumming and morris dancing. Mumming or guising was particularly strong during the late nineteenth and early twentieth century, and is currently enjoying a revival in the folk song clubs, who follow the traditional story closely, and often perform the play in local public houses. The nineteenth-century mummers took their play to local public houses and performed it at private houses also. The players acted out a legendary tale, with stock characters such as St George, Bold Hector, Slasher, Beelzebub, the Doctor and the Prince. Between them they perform a pantomime of death and resurrection in which the valiant St George is killed by Hector, and brought back to life by the Doctor. Meanwhile Black Prince and Slasher act as seconds for the battle and Beelzebub wanders on and off, putting in the odd comment and requesting pennies from the audience. F. W. Hackwood saw one of the Black Country versions performed in a Wednesbury tavern in 1879. The players were wearing the customary apparel 'and fantastically dressed in paper and tinsel, and coloured rags; some with blacked and some with floured faces; some wearing masks; some with false beards and wigs. The combat was done with broad-bladed wooden swords, with the flat of which a good sounding whack could be given'.

The introduction was made by Open-the-Door who appears once to announce:

> The first that doth step in is good old Open-the-Door,
> And, lads, if you'll believe me well, I've opened many a score.
> (With sly wink and gesture at this. He next proceeds to clear an open space for the other actors, who have now followed him in, but leave him in the centre of the stage.)

Open-the-Door proceeds to call for room, adding various other remarks, and ending with:

> Now give an eye,
> To see and hear our queer, quaint comico-tragedie.

He makes way for St George, who announces himself, boasting of his many deeds and ending with the announcement of his slaying the 'dread dragon'. On these words Bold Hector enters, wishing to know who this upstart is that claims so many deeds; then declares that he will 'always win the game'. The seconds, Slasher and Black Prince, arrive and discuss the forthcoming battle between St George and Bold Hector. Then, after a brief appearance by Beelzebub and the Blue Dwarf, the battle takes place. Hector is wounded and falls to the ground. The doctor is called and soon makes Hector rise up to:

> Sing that fine old song
> Of one who's not been dead for very long.

Hector rises and thanks the Doctor, before singing some popular song of the day, whereupon Beelzebub enters to deliver the final speech, exhorting the audience to show their appreciation with donations. He points out that Hector was revived without medicine and ends:

For your fun 'twas he fought, and got himself slain,
For your money he'll rise and fight his battles o'er again.
We hope this nonsense your spirits will joyful rouse,
So we bid you Good-day, and Peace be on this noble house!

The company of mummers then join hands and dance round singing another popular contemporary song. It is followed by another, and they march out singing, as Beelzebub collects the money in his frying-pan. The play was found throughout the County and there are a number of similar versions that have been noted intact, which vary little from the Wednesbury text in characterisation and plot.

Carols were a part of many Christmas activities and the tradition of singing and passing them on to the young was particularly strong in Staffordshire. There were few carols that were not sung in the County and collections like *A Good Christmas Box,* printed in Dudley in the mid-nineteenth century, evidence many that were not well known in other areas. Lawley tells us that:

The practice of the 'carol singers' in the Black Country is for them to wait until the bells have ended their 'merry midnight peal' before they sally forth, and then to commence their carols at the houses of those most likely to bestow 'largess' in honour of the season. Some people sit up to receive them, and treat them liberally with 'cakes and ale'. Generally, however, after singing a carol the 'waits' pass on, and call again for the customary donation when the house is astir preparing for the Christmas dinner.

In addition to the waits, carols were also sung by family groups, as part of their Christmas entertainment, and during the church ceremonies. The ever popular carols were those like 'The Sunny Bank' that had simple stories, easily remembered tunes and repetitious words:

> As I sat on the sunny bank,
> As I sat on the sunny bank,
> As I sat on the sunny bank,
> > On Christmas Day in the morning.

First lines are sung three times throughout.

> I spied three ships come sailing by,
>> On Christmas Day in the morning.

> And who should be in these three ships,
>> But Joseph and his fair lady.

> O he did whistle and she did sing,
> And all the bells on earth did ring,
> For joy our Saviour he was born
>> On Christmas Day in the morning.

Words like these were readily learned by the children who, mimicking the waits, went from door to door in the days before Christmas, singing their little store of carols and finishing each performance with a ditty that ran something like this:

> Christmas is coming the goose is getting fat
> Please put a penny in the old man's hat.
> If you hav'nt got a penny a happeny will do,
> If you hav'nt got a happeny God bless you.

This verse and many of the carols are still used by Staffordshire children for their carol-singing jaunts. The more intricate and, perhaps, interesting Christmas carols were often the special province of the few older folk, who were the carriers of folk-song proper. These carols were sung less often, but were treated with reverence by singer and audience alike. Such a carol was 'Dives and Lazarus', a lengthy didactic piece with a tricky but satisfying melody:

As it fell out upon a day,
Rich Dives made a feast,
And he invited all his friends,
And gentry of the best.

Then Lazarus laid him down and down,
E'en down at Dives door;
Some meat some drink brother Dives,
Bestow upon the poor.

Thou art none of my brother, Lazarus,
That lie begging at my door,
No meat nor drink will I give thee,
Nor bestow upon the poor.

Then Lazarus laid him down and down,
E'en down at Dives wall,
Some meat some drink brother Dives,
Or with hunger starve I shall.

Thou art none of my brother Lazarus,
That lies begging at my wall,
Neither meat nor drink shall I give thee,
But with hunger starve you shall.

Then Lazarus laid him down and down,
E'en down at Dives gate,
Some meat some drink brother Dives,
For Jesus Christ his sake.

Thou art none of my brother Lazarus,
That lies begging at my gate,
No meat nor drink will I give thee,
For Jesus Christ his sake.

Then Dives sent out his merry men,
To whip poor Lazarus away,
They had not power to strike one stroke,
But flung their whips away.

Then Dives sent out his hungry dogs,
To bite him as he lay,
They had not Pow'r to bite one bite,
But lick'd his sore away.

As it fell out upon a day,
Poor Lazarus sicken'd and died,
There came two angels out of heaven,
His soul therein to guide.

Rise up, rise up brother Lazarus,
And go along with we,
For there's a place provided in heaven,
To sit on an angel's knee.

As it fell out upon a day,
Rich Dives sicken'd and died,
There came two serpents out of hell,
His soul therein to guide.

Rise up, rise up brother Dives,
And go along with we,
For there is a place provided in hell,
To sit on a serpent's knee.

Then Dives look'd up with his eyes,
And saw poor Lazarus blest;
Give me one drop of water brother Lazarus
To quench my flaming thirst.

Oh! had I as many years to abide,
As there are blades of grass,
Then there would be an ending day,
But in hell forever must last.

Oh! was I now but alive again,
The space of one half hour,
I'd make my peace and so secure,
That the devil shou'd have no pow'r.

Finally, there were a number of events and customs that carried
the spirit of Christmas from the old year to the new, and from
Christmas past to Christmas present. Both wassailing and the Abbots
Bromley Horn Dance were features of pre-Christmas and Christmas
activities and both occurred in January; they are fully described in
the section dealing with that month; the Horn Dance is further
described in the September section. Likewise a number of towns held

their Christmas hiring-fairs, when the farm and domestic workers were hired for the coming year; in North Staffordshire one such fair was known as 'Gorby Market'. We complete this look at the Turning Year with a glance at the custom of keeping the yule log from one year to the next. In Staffordshire it was once common for every family to burn a yule log. It remained alight throughout the Christmas night festivities, when it was quenched and the remains set aside to light the next Christmas Yule log. While the custom of burning a yule log was on the decline in the late nineteenth century, it was still practised by many.

7   Local Humour

APART FROM the varied humour revolving round the towns and villages of Staffordshire, there are many jokes concerned with individuals: the story of the bishop and the kettle is a good example.

A group of Bilston colliers were returning from work one day when they saw a hawker's cart approaching. It was moving along slowly: all the pots, pans and kettles were bouncing, shaking and rattling in response to every rut and hole in the road. As it passed by the colliers the cart went through a particularly big rut: it bounced high in the air and a kettle was thrown on the road. The hawker did not notice his loss and the cart continued on its way. When it was safely out of sight, the colliers picked up the kettle and wondered who should take it and how they should select him. One of the colliers suggested they should sit on a nearby wall and tell tall tales; the biggest liar would win the kettle. The competition was well under way by the time Bishop Selwyn came along the road. Seeing the colliers laughing and joking, the Bishop stopped his carriage, climbed down and asked what was afoot. The colliers explained what they were doing and the Bishop was very shocked: 'Why, my dear fellows, lying is a dreadful sin. My mother made me promise when I was a boy that I would never tell a lie, and I never have.'

At this the group of colliers burst into laughter and one of them called out: 'Gi' the Bishop the kettle; he's won it fair.' The Bishop, who could not win in this Black Country style of humour, climbed back in his carriage and drove off, leaving the colliers kicking the kettle about the street.

A common form of joke directed at individuals and still popular was giving nick-names generally based on some physical characteristic. At one time many people were known exclusively by their nick-names, so it sometimes happened that they themselves did not know their original names. Accounts of weddings, where the vicar was unable to proceed with the ceremony for want of a proper name, occur in various nineteenth-century papers. A writer in a local newspaper recalls one man who was unable to give his real name in court, because he had known himself by his nick-name since early childhood. His name was eventually supplied by a friend, who had come with him. A miscellaneous newspaper report from the early twentieth century described the following anecdote:

One of the most comical specimens of Black Country nicknaming appeared some time ago in a local sporting publication, and is well worthy of reproduction here. A solicitor's clerk was sent to serve a process on one of these oddly named individuals but failed to find the object of his search and was giving up the task as hopeless when a young woman who had witnessed his labours volunteered her help. 'Oi say, Bullyed,' cried she to the first person they met, 'does thee know a man named Adam Green?' The bullhead was shaken in token of ignorance. 'Loy-a-bed, does thee know?' 'Lie-a-bed' could not answer either. 'Stumpy' (a man with a wooden leg), 'Cowskin', 'Spindleshanks', 'Cockeye', and 'Pigtail' were successively consulted to no purpose. At length, however, having had conversation with several friends, the damsel's eyes suddenly brightened, and slapping one of her neighbours on the shoulder she exclaimed: 'Dash my wig, woy he means moy faythur.' Then turning to the astonished clerk, she cried, 'You should have ax'd for 'O'd Blackbird.'

Staffordshire has many anecdotes of one town claiming precedence over another and there are few better stories than that of the red hot shilling. Legend has it that a Bilstonian was visiting nearby Darlaston on business. As he neared the town centre he heard a general hubbub and, turning a corner, encountered a large crowd gathered as if they were watching a cock-fight. Turning to the nearest of the crowd, he asked what was going on, and learned that a unique object had been found lying on the ground. The watchers had gathered round, though they were keeping at a safe distance. The traveller asked the crowd to let him through, pointing out that he was widely travelled and might be able to recognise this strange thing. The cry went up 'make room for the stranger' and very soon he was looking at a gold sovereign. Turning to the crowd, he started to say, 'Why it's only a ....' Then, seeing they really had no idea what it was, never having seen such a large sum of money in one piece, he said, 'It's only a red hot shilling.' A mutter went up from the crowd and one man voiced all their fears, when he suggested it was brought by the Devil. The stranger quickly told them it was really a good shilling: they would have to wait until it cooled before they could pick it up. Then he said, 'I'll tell you what I'll do. I've got plenty of time and nothing much to do, so I'll give you one of my shillings. While you go off and enjoy yourself, I'll wait for this one to cool and then pick it up.'

A cheer went up from the assembled crowd. One of the men pocketed the shilling and off they went to the local pub. As they made off one or two looked back to wave at the stranger and saw him seated comfortably reading a book and occasionally putting a hand out to test the heat from the shilling. Eventually the last of the crowd disappeared. The stranger immediately picked up the sovereign and made off towards Bilston whistling to himself.

Opportunities to have a dig at a nearby town or village were seldom missed. It was said that, on one occasion, the Wednesfield men ran short of beef at a wake. A visitor remarked that they had only killed half a bull and were keeping the other half for the next wake. A man who lived in Darlaston was said to own a pig from which rashers could be cut while it was alive: the flesh renewed itself within a short time. Similar stories are told in other regions.

We have already seen, in the chapter on the Devil, that the characteristics of a village or town, real or imagined, can be the subject of verse and taunt. When the reactions of the Devil were not relevant, people were quick to seize on other means of expressing their amusement. Often such verses mentioned more than one town, as in:

> Stramshall and Bramshall,
> Beamhurst and Fold,
> Leachurch and Parkhurst,
> And Chetley i' th' hole.

The rhyme might simply call attention to some feature of town or village without an attempt at humour:

> The stoutest beggar that goes by the way,
> Can't beg through Long on a midsummer's day.

Long is Longden near Lichfield, once well known for the length of its main street. Natural and man-made objects were responsible for a variety of proverbial sayings, connected with specific villages. In North Staffordshire a village called Narrow Dale near Onecote gave rise to the saying: 'It must be done in a Narrow Dale moon – now or never.' Narrow Dale is surrounded by tall rocks, and it was said that inhabitants never saw the sun in winter, and only for a short time at noon on summer days. Thus any job needing to be done quickly had to be done in a Narrow Dale moon. 'Short as a Marchington Wake cake' is taken to mean something that is very nice, but of which there is not enough. Presumably a slight at Marchington for baking a mean, though tasty, wake cake was intended. Still in common use is the saying 'All the way round the Wrekin', which means someone who has taken the long route round, or someone who is long-winded in speech; the Wrekin is an extensive hill in Shropshire. At Baswich the Weeping Cross gave rise to the saying 'He's returned by Weeping Cross', meaning someone who has repented of a misdeed.

Perhaps the commonest form of local humour was concerned with village taunts directed at one village by the residents of another. These vary. They may be verses concerned with one town like:

Woton under Weaver
Where God came never.

which refers to the bleakness of the district surrounding the village.
Similarly:

A tumble-down church,
A tottering steeple,
A drunken parson,
And a wicked people.

—being a reference to Willenhall. At nearby Walsall the local vicar
was criticized by some local wit, who wrote:

Our new church, our old steeple,
Our proud parson, our poor people.

The lines are said to refer to the restoration of the church, the
poverty of the majority of the population, and the austerity of the
vicar's life.

Most of the village taunts tend to be verses that refer to certain
places, such as:

Caldon, Calton, Waterfall, and Grin,
Four of the foulest towns ever man was in.

—and similarly:

Tamworth and Uttoxeter—
Both sold the Church Bible to buy a town bear.

Other rhymes direct different insults at each town they mention:

Walsall for bandy legs,
Baggeridge for nuts,
Bilston for dust and dirt,
And Sedgley for sluts.

Some verses praise one town and insult another. Presumably the authors were partisan:

> Sutton for mutton,
> Tanworth for beef,
> Wasall for bandy legs,
> And Brum for a thief.

Neighbouring villages taunted Darlaston folk: they had two Sundays in the year when they did not put a pot on the fire for dinner. One was Wake Sunday, when they roasted the meat; the other was the Sunday after, when they had nothing to boil. The eating habits of the entire Black Country area are summed up in this rhyme, which suggests that its people were unable to budget properly. They were improvident at the beginning of the week and penniless at the end:

Sunday	— Hot meat day
Monday	— Cold Meat day
Tuesday	— Hash day
Wednesday	— Cabbage and bacon day
Thursday	— Bread and cheese day
Friday	— Clam day
Saturday	— Getting drunk day

There is a rhyme known in several counties which is most insulting to Staffordshire: a quean was a hussie:

> Nottingham full of hogs,
> Derbyshire full of dogs,
> Leicestershire full of beans,
> Staffordshire full of queans.

To complete the town and village rhymes, here is a verse from the east of the county. It lists various villages and ends with a quip at the expense of Tamworth, 'the head town':

> There's Bitterscote and Bonehill,
> And Dunstall upon Dunn,
> Hopwas and Coton,
> And miry Wigginton;
> Little Amington and Great Amington,

With the Woodhouses by,
Glascote and Wilncote,
And merry Faseley;
Comberford and Syerscote,
And Bole Hall Street –
And Tamworth is the head town,
Where all the cuckolds meet.

No look at Staffordshire humour would be complete without mentioning those two famous Black Country characters, Aynuck and Ayli. They embody the Black Country spirit and feature in most local jokes. Many sayings are attributed to them: 'Some men are like Bilston mines – theer's good stuff in them if you could only get them dry, but they'm always soaked.' Their wise sayings cover just about all community activity. Even preachers are ridiculed: 'I like a preacher to knock off when he's done. Too many on 'em go on ten minutes after they've finished.'

They are as popular today as they were fifty years ago and, when joke-telling sessions take place in South Staffordshire pubs, a good proportion of them will be Aynuck and Ayli jokes; their names are spelt in a variety of ways. Apart from their comments and jokes on domestic, social and working life they are also politically conscious and interpret attitudes towards schemes like the Channel Tunnel. The Black Country joke about the Channel Tunnel was put into verse by a local rhymester more than ten years ago: the song has become a 'traditional' piece for those who listen to it. Putting a pig on a wall to watch the band going by is a reference to an Old Black Country joke aimed at the Gornal folk and is intended to set the scene for this modern exploit:

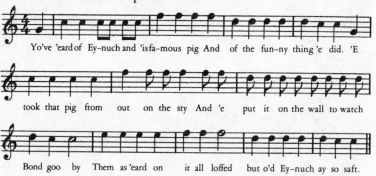

Yo've 'eard of Ey-nuch and 'is fa-mous pig And of the fun-ny thing 'e did. 'E took that pig from out on the sty And 'e put it on the wall to watch Bond goo by Them as 'eard on it all loffed but o'd Ey-nuch ay so saft.

Yo've 'eard of Aynuck an' 'is famous pig
And of the funny thing 'e did:
'E took that pig from out on the sty,
And 'e put it on the wall to watch the bond (band) goo by.

Chorus:
Them as 'eard on it all loffed (laughed),
But owd Aynuck ay so saft (soft).

A clever kid was owd Aynuck,
An' at engineerin' 'e tried 'is luck.
The Gover'ment thought 'e was gi'in 'em the flannel
When 'e said 'e'd dig a tunnel under the Channel.

'Ow'm yo gonna do it?' the Prime Minister said.
Says Aynuck, 'I'll dig off Beachy 'Ead.
But I wo 'ave to dig too far!' he cried,
'Cos ower kid's diggin' from the other side.'

'Aynuck, you're talking in a riddle,
What if you miss him in the middle?'
Aynuck says: 'Kid, yo'm easy on!
Yo'll 'ave two tunnels instead o' one.'

8 The Working Day

THE 'KNOCKERS', those little folk who helped or hindered and were playful or malicious as the whim took them, were described in detail in the earlier chapter about supernatural beings. The taps of the 'knockers' were not the only means by which the colliers were warned of impending disaster. One of the most potent and feared of these portents were Gabriel's Hounds. Plot encountered them in the late eighteenth century. Writing in his *Natural History of Staffordshire,* he says:

> We need go no farther for an instance than the same *Town* of *Wednesbury,* where the *Colyers* will tell you that early in the morning as they go to their work, and from the *Cole-pits* themselves, they sometimes hear the noise of a *pack* of *hounds* in the *Air,* which has happened so frequently that they have got a name for them, calling them *Gabriels hounds,* though the more sober and judicious take them only to be *Wild-geese,* making this noise in their *flight;*

If Gabriel's Hounds were heard, the boldest of colliers refused to work; likewise, if there was a hearing, or reported hearing, of the Seven Whistlers, a disaster warning which resembled Gabriel's Hounds. The Seven Whistlers made bird-like cries overhead, or near the mouth of a pit. If they were overhead, the miners would turn back from work. If they were near the pit-head, the men left and went home. Hearing the Hounds or the Whistlers meant that a pit explosion or pit-fall would soon take place, leading to serious injury or loss of life. Nor would the colliers go on to work if they met a cross-eyed woman or a one-legged man, or saw a robin perched on a wall, or a pump or some other artificial object; if the robin perched on a natural object such as a tree or rock, then no danger would follow. It was also unlucky to let the fire go out or find an old shoe, though, if the finder could hide the shoe without being seen, the danger would be averted.

In her book *Black Country Sketches,* Amy Lyons recalls that the Cockfighters Arms at Old Moxley, once the haunt of pitmen and pit-bank girls, used to have a large board over the chimney-piece in the tap room. On it was painted:

YE COLLIER'S GUIDE OF SIGNES AND WARNINGS

1st – To dreame of a broken shoe, a sure signe of danger.

2nd – If you mete a woman at the rising of ye sun turne again from ye pit, a sure signe of deathe.

3rd – To dream of a fire is a signe of danger.

4th – To see a bright light in ye mine is a warninge to flee away.

5th – If Gabriel's Hounds ben aboute, doe no work that day.

6th – When foule smells be about ye pit, a sure signe that ye imps ben annear.

7th – To charme away ghostes and ye like: Take a Bible and a Key, hold both in ye right hand, and saye ye Lord's Prayer, and they will right speedily get farre away.

Lawley, in his *Staffordshire Folklore,* quotes an old Sedgley document, where an item dated 1711 states:

Some colliers going to work in Mr Peroehouse's Colliery at Moorfield, near Ettingshall, met a woman. As it was sunrise they became alarmed, and some of them turned back. Several others went to work laughing at such fears. In less than two hours an explosion of fire-damp occurred, and a man was killed.

It was also a general custom, certainly in the south of the County, for colliers not to work a pit where a fatal accident had taken place until the dead had been buried. They believed that the spirit of the dead roamed at large prior to the burial. In the late nineteenth century the Rowley Regis Colliery Company prosecuted six of their miners at Old Hill Police Court for neglect of work. The company claimed that the men had signed an agreement not to observe the custom, except in the pit where an accident had occurred. The men were eventually discharged on payment of costs.

Stealing from the body of a dead comrade also met with serious results, since the spirit of the dead person would not be able to rest until the stolen article had been returned. It would haunt the mine, waiting for the thief to admit his guilt, return the item, and make suitable apology to the bereft family.

We have already seen in chapter 6 that the colliers performed morris dances at May time. They also used morris dancing as a means of raising cash when they were on strike. At such times they would make up songs to accompany their strike activities. In about 1860 the colliers of South Staffordshire had one such song, though we now have only the burden, which ran:

> O, the shilling!
> O, the shilling!
> We'd sooner starve
> Than go to work
> At a shilling a day!

An earlier, more complete and interesting song known as *The Brave Collier Lads* appears to have derived from a piece known as *Shepherd's Song*. The scene is still set in the countryside and the young maiden is a milkmaid. But her father and her lover-to-be are colliers, and a condition made by the girl, for her acceptance of the young collier's advances, is that he should be a member of 'the union'. The song first appeared in print in its collier form in the mid-eighteenth century, though its content indicates some purposeful interference by union enthusiasts during the early and mid-nineteenth century. Our

Staffordshire version comes without a tune, though the music for *Shepherd's Song,* in the English Folk Dance and Song Society's Publication *Marrow Bones* (p. 78), is easily adapted:

As I walked forth one summer's morn, all in the month of June
The flowers they were springing and the birds were in full tune,
I overheard a lovely maid and this was all her theme,
'Success attend the collier lads, for they are lads of fame.'

I stepped up to her and bending on my knee
I asked her pardon for making with her so free:
'My pardon it is granted, young collier' she replies;
'Pray do you belong to the brave Union boys?'

'You may say I'm a collier, as black as a sloe;
And all night long I am working down below.'
'Oh, I do love a collier as I do love my life –
My father was a pitman all the days of his life.'

'Come now my young collier and rest here awhile,
And when I've done milking, I'll give you a smile.'
He kissed her sweet lips while milking her cow;
And the lambs they were sporting all in the morning dew.

'Come all you noble gentlemen, wherever you may be,
Do not pull down their wages, nor break their unity;
You see they hold like brothers, like sailors on the sea,
They do their best endeavours for their wives and family.'

Then she clapt her arms around him, like Venus round the vine,
'You are my jolly collier lad, you've won this heart of mine,
And if that you do win the day, as you have won my heart,
I'll crown you with honour and forever take your part.'

The colliers are the best boys, their lives underground,
And when they to the ale house go they value not a crown;
They spend their money freely and pay before they go,
They work underground while the stormy winds do blow.

'So come all you pretty maids, wherever you may be,
A collier lad do not despise in any degree,
For if that you do use them well they'll do the same to thee;
There is none in this world like a pit boy for me.'

This timely adaptation was not only found in Staffordshire – it appeared on broadsides from various parts of the country. The printers obviously found the struggles of the colliers and other industrial groups a lucrative business, since many workers' strike songs and verses explaining their plight to the rest of society appeared on commercial broadsides as everyday street literature. These broadsides and privately printed and/or financed broadsides could also be used as a means to raise cash for the strike fund, through sales made by the striking group. *The Brave Collier Lads* was only one of a number of colliers' songs that appeared on Staffordshire broadsides. Similarly, the nail-makers of South Staffordshire and North Worcestershire produced a fairly extensive number of songs that were written for broadside circulation or eventually found their way on to broadsides. The nail-makers composed songs on various topics; those describing the day-to-day problems of the trade and their families, those concerned with exhorting them to carry on with the struggle whatever the cost, and songs about specific strikes.

The Nail Strike is an example of the third category – a song believed to date from 1862, when the nailers went on a strike that lasted twenty weeks. One of their strike activities was to print and distribute this song to explain their case. They distributed it as they marched from Netherton to Bromsgrove, hauling a heavy tub of coal, given by a well-wisher, to show their willingness to work for fair wages. The march and strike were led by Sam Salt, shopowner, book-seller and poet, who also wrote a one hundred and five verse poem stating the nailers' case. When the marchers arrived at Bromsgrove, where they planned to talk with the nail masters, they sold the coal to provide money for the strikers. The strike was successful, in so far as the masters eventually passed a resolution that offered the men the

opportunity of returning to their work at the 20s rate for a period of two months; with the understanding that in the meantime they endeavour to induce the masters in the up-districts to pay the same. Should the up-district masters decline to do so the Bromsgrove masters will then reduce to what they are paying.

Bromsgrove and Droitwich Weekly Messenger,

1 August 1863

The nailers took the offer, which proved to be a very temporary restraint in the downward spiral of their wages and conditions:

> You nailmakers all that day remember well,
> In the last strike of which this tale I tell,
> How cold and hungry we that heavy day,
> To Bromsgrove town did take our toilsome way.
>
> And these Nailforgers miserable souls,
> Will not forget the givers of the coals,
> Nail masters are hard-hearted files,
> The way we took was thirteen miles.
>
> Oh the slaves abroad in the sugar canes,
> Find plenty to help and pity their pains,
> But the slaves at home in the mine and fire,
> Find plenty to pity but none to admire.
>
> Oh I wish I could see all Nail Dealers,
> Draw such a load as did we poor Nailors,
> And to feel such punishment and such smart,
> That it may soften their hard stony hearts.
>
> So as the Nailors do suffer such smart,
> I hope it will soften old Pharoah's heart,
> And let every nailor tell to his son,
> The labours that we for our rights have done.

Further north the potters had their own problems. The use of machinery in certain processes of their trade was creating difficulties. Unlike the nailers, who were unaware of the encroachment of the machine into their lives, the potters were very conscious of its presence. The nailers worked in small family units, in their own houses, and the new nail manufactories developed in non-traditional nailing areas, so that the hand-nailers only knew of the machines by hearsay; whereas the potters already worked in extensive potteries, and the machines were introduced into them. The one that caused most trouble was the 'jolly' machine. The Children's Employment Commission reported:

In some manufactories machines called 'heads' or 'jollies' are used
for the manufacture of the more common shapes of round ware.
The ware is formed in moulds which are turned by steam-power;
a lump of clay is placed in the mould, and the cup or bowl is
formed by the pressure of a piece of iron upon the clay while the
mould is revolving. By means of these simple machines children
and women are employed as substitutes for the skilled
thrower . . . .

Unlike the 'machine wreckers' of the Luddite era, the potters did
not take unofficial violent action, but the unions watched the
situation keenly and individuals put pen to paper to record their
objections in song. In *The Jolly Machine,* the writer draws attention
to the ill-fated weavers (a 'spattler' is a nineteenth-century term for
a strike-breaking machine operator):

I'll sing you a song of a 'Jolly' machine
Which Potters all say is a rattler
And excells every other, as yet, ever seen
I'm sure you'll pronounce it a 'spattler'.

I am quite in earnest so pray lend an ear
My song it is true and no folly
As from this machine you have too much to fear
It's a thief that I call master 'Jolly'.

A thief did I call it? aye, well you may stare
But prove it I can and most fully
For if it deprives you of making crock ware
Why, what will become of your belly?

It makes bowls and plates in such mighty big 'rucks'
Believe me, I'm no lying sinner
And I'm told, by and by, he'll make all our cups
Then what shall we do for a dinner?

That 'Jolly's' a robber, deny it who can
And brings on distress the most heavy
But how to avert it I'll tell every man
Why, down with his half-crown levy.

Some selfish one's tell us that 'Jolly' won't act,
I think they are greatly mistaken
It is only to save their half-crown that's a fact
And care not for other men's bacon.

If the fate of the weaver you would avert
And ward off destruction so heavy
Why come forward like men, that will not be hurt
And pay down your half-a-crown levy.

Apart from wage rates and the problem of machines, there were other factors that created discontent among Staffordshire's industrial workers. Perhaps the most hated facet of industrial life was the Truck System whereby workers were paid in full, or part, by company notes, sometimes known as tommy notes. These could only be exchanged at the company shop, or other shops designated by the company, where the goods were frequently low in quality and high in price compared with the open market. Even after the Truck Acts the system continued to flourish, and nowhere more so than in South Staffordshire. It is a strange fact that, as hated as it was, the Truck System was seldom mentioned in industrial balladry and there are few, if any, other songs that devote the whole of their content to the subject as in the *Tommy Note*. Stranger still, the *Tommy Note* is the only song about the working life of the canal people that has been discovered to date; other songs about canals are concerned with the social life of canal people, though these are fairly sparce. That it should be the only industrial ballad about the canal folk and the Truck System is doubly strange. It appeared on a Birmingham broadside printed in the mid-nineteenth century and, like many of its counterparts, has survived without its melody. It must have circulated quite widely among the canal folk of Staffordshire and elsewhere in the Midland Counties, though it has never been reported from any other source. A selection of its seven verses are quoted here:

You Boatsmen and colliers all,
Come listen to my ditty,
I'll sing you a song before its long,
It is both new and pretty;

It is concerning tommy shops,
And the high field* ruffian
He pays you with a tommy note,
You must have that or nothing
    Fal de riddle ral.

When they have done their runcan† voyage,
And go to receive their money,
One half stops for hay and corn
The other half for tommy,
Then to the tommy shops we go,
To fetch our week's provision,
Their oatmeal, sugar, salt and soap,
Short weight and little measure.
    Fal de riddle ral.

Now we have finished our voyage,
The children look so funny,
For here at runcan we do lie,
And have eat all our tommy,
Come gear the horse and clear the line,
And jump on board the boat sir,
Both night and day we'll steer our way,
For another tommy note sir.
    Fal de riddle ral.

* Highfield, probably a district of Wolverhampton.
† runcan, Runcorn, Cheshire.

This 'floating' population had its own traditional forms of entertainment as well, and it seems likely that they devoted much more of their time to enjoyable pub sing-song and melodeon playing than to writing 'protest songs' and worrying about the industrial situation in which they found themselves. Few writers have penetrated the real social life of the canal people. L.T.C. Rolt spent much of his time on the canals and came to know particular groups well. Here he is writing in his book *The Inland Waterways of England*:

I recall one memorable evening at a canal pub . . . . It consisted mainly of boatmen and gypsies . . . . It was not long before there were calls for 'the music', and a melodeon, the instrument which most boatmen favoured, was produced. Though none of those present could read a note of music, each of the boatmen took his turn as musician. The repertoire is always the same. Apart from a few lively 'stepping tunes' such as 'Cock o' the North' it is drawn almost exclusively from the nineteenth-century heyday of music hall . . . . Each of the boatmen, one of them over seventy, performed a step dance, footing it with remarkable agility and sense of rhythm in their heavy hobnailed boots . . . .

One of the industries that produced little in the way of industrial balladry was the iron industry. This massive employer of labour has produced only one song in Staffordshire – a paean of praise for the great Black Country iron-master, John Wilkinson. Wilkinson's Black Country iron-works were situated at Bilston and Bradley, but he had others in Shropshire, and near Wrexham, and the words of his song were tailored to fit the works in the Black Country and near Wrexham. It was popular in about 1780, a time when it was not uncommon to find songs praising the benevolent employer, but unusual to find adverse criticism:

> You workmen of Bilston and Bradley draw near,
> Sit down, take your pipes and my song you shall hear.
> I sing not of war or the state of the nation,
> Such subjects as these produce nought but vexation.

The song suggests a toast to Wilkinson's health and prosperity, and continues:

> That the wood of Old England would fail, did appear
> And though iron was scarce because charcoal was dear,
> By puddling and stamping he cured that evil,
> So the Swedes and the Russians may go to the divil.

> Our thundering cannon too frequently burst,
> A mischief so great he prevented the first.
> And now it is well known they never miscarry,
> But drive all our foes with a blast to old Harry.

> Then let each jolly fellow take hold of his glass,
> And drink to the health of his friend and his lass.
> May we always have plenty of good beer and pence,
> And Wilkinson's fame blaze a thousand years hence.

There are quite a number of Staffordshire customs, rhymes and songs connected with industry in general, rather than with specific groups or industries. The payment of 'footings' or 'foot ale' by those starting to learn a new trade, or those visiting works and handling the tools of the trade was once common; the amount exacted was spent on ale, as the term implies. Two rhymes from Mrs E. M. Turner of Wednesbury also give some evocative and amusing insights into the early morning activities of workmen making ready:

Early in the morning when the cock begins to crow
Off to work you know our father has to go.
With his little nosebag a plodding through the rain
We shout "Good Morning, father" and we go to sleep again.

and:

Stop that clock or I'll lose a quarter
Doe lie snoring on yer back.
If I'm not there to mix the mortar,
On me word I'll get the sack.
Bridget doe yer stop to dress yer,
Doe yer stop to put on yer frock,
But while I'm pulling up me trousers
Ye goo down and stop that clock.

The patriotic and rousing *Song of the Staffordshire Men* may well come from a literary pen, although it could be the work of a late nineteenth-century workman or craftsman, educated at a mechanic's institute, or the like. It is the only Staffordshire song to unite the thoughts and feelings of the north and south of the county; one of the pecularities of this area is the cultural, as well as geographical, separation of the Black Country and the Potteries. The men of the Potteries not only live closer to the Lancashire folk, they also share their social and cultural outlook. But this song unites the two areas and praises the men, the products they make, and the land they were born into:

There's many a task for the English folk,
And a man's a man alway;

Who delves the coal and iron ore,
And shapes the potters' clay.

Chorus: For this is the song of the Staffordshire men,
In forge, in kiln, in mine,
Our fires shall burn, and our mill-wheels turn,
And the knot shall be our sign.

There are forty shires that light their fires,
And bless the iron strong,
And the china bake the potters make,
As they sing the Stafford song.

We come of a race of yeomen bold,
Whose drink is the best of beer;
Our fields feed beasts for the Christmas feast
And you may share our (Staffordshire) cheer.

We marshal our ranks on the grey pit banks
And our lads on the football field,
If the cause be right, we are game to fight,
We never were known to yield.

The humour of Aynuck and Ayli has been mentioned in an earlier chapter. These two Black Country legendary characters have been folk heroes since the early nineteenth century at least, and their popularity shows no sign of waning at the present time; if anything, they are now better established and more popular than they have ever been. Their adventures, sayings, tales, jokes, stories and poems reflect the true tenacity, strength of purpose and single-mindedness that marks the regions' people, and they are not just remembered through the folk process, but form a crucial ingredient in the present day social and working life. Like all good heroes, they can also take a joke against themselves and much of the humour surrounding them is of this type, as we have seen in the chapter on *Local Humour.* Today they are the men who have the answer to everything, whose skills are innumerable, their lives immortal. Historically, in the folk poem *'O'd Aynuck,* they are in turn nailer, chainmaker, collier, iron worker;

Our Eynuch bay quite jed,
Nor niver wull be,

Our Eynuch bay fergot,
Nor niver con be.
Tek a sank around Blackheath,
Or down the tump an' in't o'd 'Ills.
Stond annunst the cross fer 'arf-an-hour
Just t'watch the Folken all goo by.
Yoh'll see 'im theer as big as life,
O'd Eynuch, our Eynuch.

Our Eynuch left 'is mark,
Yoh can't mistaike et, see?
'Is 'ommer prints bin 'ere
An always wull be.
Just look in all the nail shops,
If some bay the'er that meks no odds.
See that ooman scruven up the gledes?
That's 'er wot fashions all the nails,
Yoh'll bet 'er mon bay fer away,
O'd Eynuch, our Eynuch.

Our Eynuch med big chains
(Is ooman med small).
See them the'er big anchors?
Eynuch med 'um all.
In Cradley Heath you'll find 'im
Around any chain shop in the day,
Or if it's night look in the pubs
(Yoh'll see 'um nustled 'gainst the cherch)
O'd Eynuch, our Eynuch.

No Eynuch bay quite jed,
Nor 'e niver wull be,
O'd Eynuch bay fergot,
Nor niver con be.
'Ast ever sid a Jews 'Arp?
'E med 'um all be Rowley Cherch,
Stond atop Hawes Hill an' look a'down
See all them lights annunst the cut,
He used to puddle iron the'er
O'd Eynuch, our Eynuch.

'Ommer, is a hammer, and 'scruven up the gledes' means raking out the cinders from the cold furnace or grate. The women employed to do this work in the foundries and elsewhere were known as 'gledes-women'. The partially-burnt gledes were re-used.

Another interesting group of rhymes comes from the nineteenth-century street-traders who dealt in everything, from fly-papers to besoms. The watercress-sellers could frequently be heard about the Staffordshire streets and towns delivering their sing-song sales-talk. A verse used at Derby End ran:

> Water cress, water cress,
> Derby End water cress.
> Every ha'porth meks it less
> Who'll buy me water cress.

Close by, at Lower Gornal, the sand-sellers were frequent visitors and their catchy ditty was well known:

> Get yer sond, get yer sond,
> Ha'penny a bucket, and some in yer 'ond.

In the main the cries were simply drawn out chants, without recognisable melodic form, but the Wednesbury fly-paper sellers could boast a pretty tune for their sales piece:

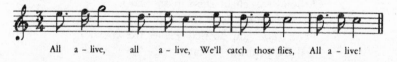

All a – live,   all   a – live, We'll catch those flies, All a – live!

The rhymes were generally short, to get the message over quickly, but the sellers of Mother Shipton's soap used this fairly lengthy cry in the Bilston area:

> Good ode mother has cum agen to wish yer joy,
> Good ode mother 'er soap yo ought to buy,
> 'Er washin' is dun with arf the werk
> 'Er soap it will soon shift all the dirt,
> Just try it at washin' a dirty shert
> Good ode mother!

The broom sellers of Great Wyrley near Cannock, had a number of chants. One ran:

> Buy a broom, buy a broom,
> There's a big one for the lady,
> But a small one for the baby,
> So all you good folks
> Will you buy a broom.

At one time Wyrley Common was covered with gorse broom. When the plant was in bloom, it was gathered and made into brooms, which were hawked around the Black Country towns by the womenfolk of 'Worley Bonk' or Great Wyrley. Early in the morning a train of donkeys would leave Wyrley and one by one the vendors would leave the train to take up their separate selling areas. The women were renowned for their colourful clothing, broadness of language and wild disposition. The donkeys rivalled in local fame the Gornal sand donkeys. The opening of the collieries on the common, and competition created by the manufacture of brooms by prison inmates, killed off the ancient craft. They also sang:

> Buy my brooms, my bonny brooms,
> If yo' wantin' any;
> Come buy 'em, come buy 'em,
> They'm only a penny.

> Come buy 'em, come buy 'em,
> My bonny new brooms,
> They'm only a penny,
> To sweep up your rooms.

> They're fresh from the common,
> The best ever seen,
> The dew ain't dry on 'em,
> They'm sweet and clean.

> Come buy 'em, come buy 'em,
> My bonny new brooms,
> A penny I axes
> To sweep up yer rooms.

> Buy my brooms, bonny brooms.

Lawley recalls that the broom women who sang this song called at his mother's home and adds that the song was sung to 'a simple air in a sweet voice, in no despicable manner, to which when we were young we used to listen, and imitate, though their pronunciation was of the broadest'.

The Burton-on-Trent barrel race is a recently revived trade custom. On Sunday 27th June, 1976, it was held in Burton High Street for the first time in forty years. Over thirty teams took part, rolling the barrels with a bobbin-stick, a traditional tool used in the breweries for moving casks.

There seem to be few beliefs or songs connected with farming in Staffordshire, apart from those mentioned in the *Turning Year* chapter. Similarly the use of charms to increase the yield of milk, and help man and beast to work harder, have also been mentioned in the chapter *Cradle to the Grave*. The County did boast two rather strange pools for which unusual properties were claimed. The first, Druid Mere, at Aldridge, was said to overflow on the approach of a year of dearth; but it remained very shallow during the years of plenty. If the pool filled, local farmers would dig holes in their fields, puddle them with clay and collect rain-water against the coming shortage.

The second, called Hungry Pool, was situated at Billingham, near Stafford. Its properties resembled those of Druid Mere: it overflowed in times of drought and was nearly empty after great rains. It was claimed that people would set up sticks in the mud and foretell the price of corn on the market by the rise and fall of water on the sticks; local farmers were said to have made a fortune by keeping a close eye on Hungry pool.

These were the only two pools that affected farmers but there were at least two others in Staffordshire that possessed marvellous features. One, of an unknown location, foretold coming events by a great roaring, and it was claimed that no wild beast would drink its water or go into it. The other was a lake known as Mahall and lay 'near Magdallen in this shire'. When hunters arrived there, tired and thirsty, they and their horses would drink the water, and shortly afterwards become as fresh 'as if they had not run at all'.

Claims of inducing rain by magical prayers are by no means unknown. The severe drought of the summer of 1976 brought out a number of rainmakers: a Staffordshire clergyman claimed to be the first and most successful. He wrote a rain prayer, which members of his congregation chanted every day for a week. At the end of the seventh day, there was a brief shower of rain. It was followed, some hours later, by a torrential downpour that lasted, on and off, for two or three days. The clergyman, the Rev. Terry Stokes, was quoted as saying that it proved the prayers offered up by his Shelfield, Walsall, parishioners had been successful: the down-pour came through his kitchen ceiling and soaked the floor.

9   Sports and Pastimes

MANY TRADITIONAL sports and pastimes were part of wakes week which, as we saw in Chapter 6 (September), began as a religious observance and ended as a time for pleasure. Besides the sports mentioned in the Newcastle Wakes song, cock-fighting, bull-baiting, boxing and wrestling became an accepted part of the wake entertainments, though each remained an independent sport in its own right until they were either banned or modified to meet the more civilised outlook of mid-nineteenth century society.

Cock-fighting was once a very popular Black Country sport and many public houses had their own cock-pits in the back yard. It is believed that the Romans introduced the sport to Britain and, apart from a brief and only partially successful ban imposed by Cromwell in 1654, its popularity continued unabated until the nineteenth century. During the last few years of the eighteenth century anti-blood sport groups began to gain support and, by the mid-nineteenth century, public opinion was clearly against the continuance of cock-fighting; it was finally banned under the Cruelty to Animals Act of 1849. From this date the large organised matches were more or less discontinued, though matches were still fought in back street pubs, cellars, disused pits, and the like, on a fairly wide scale.

Each individual owner or trainer developed his own special breeding, feeding and training techniques, which he kept a closely guarded secret. When the birds entered the cock-pit, they found themselves in a ring approximately twenty-two feet in circumference, which was surrounded by a low wall. Outside the ring the better pits were banked with seats, and the whole arena was roofed and walled. In the pit the birds were governed by strict rules and conditions. Most fights were straight forward one to one battles, but variations included the 'Battle Royal' in which a number of birds were placed in the pit simultaneously and left to fight it out; in the 'Welsh Main' a number of cocks were matched in pairs, each winner being paired with another, until only one bird was left. A main was a series of matches and it was the name applied to ordinary matches, as well as the 'Welsh Main.' Before entering the pit, the birds' natural spurs were replaced with metal ones, so that a well-aimed blow often proved fatal.

South Staffordshire and the Black Country seem to have been the area responsible for the largest number of cock-fighting songs. One of the best known was *The Wedgebury Cocking* when:

> At Wedgebury there was a cocking,
> A match between Newton and Scroggins,
> The colliers and nailers left work,
> And all to Spittle's went jogging
> To see this noble sport;
> Many noted men there resorted,
> And though they'd but little money,
> Yet that they freely sported.

The song describes how they all gather and the bets are placed. Eventually the cockers retire to lunch at Spittle's pub, where a variety of foods and events are laid on. After lunch:

> Then they all returned to the pit,
> And the fighting went forward again,
> Six battles were fought on each side,
> And the next to decide the main;

After these confrontations, the main fight of the day is held. In the event of the decision not going the right way, the sportsmen fall out with one another and a pitched battle takes place. The fight ends when:

> They trampled both cocks to death,
> And so they made a draw of the main.

It seems to have been a regular event for the sportsmen to disagree and fight over the results of the cock fights. Close by Wedgebury or Wednesbury lies Wednesfield and in *The Wednesfield Wake* a similar drama is played out, though the two birds survive to fight another day:

> At Wednesfield at one village wake,
> The cockers all did meet,
> At Billy Lane's the cockfighters,
> To have a sporting treat.
>
> For Charley Marson's spangled cock,
> Was matched to fight a red,
> That came from Wil'n'all all o'er the fields,
> And belonged to 'Cheeky Ned'.
>
> Two finer birds in any cock-pit,
> There never yet was seen.
> Though the Wednesfield man declared,
> Their cock was sure to win.
>
> The cocks fought well and feather fled
> All round about the pit,
> While blood from both of 'em did flow,
> Yet ne'er un would submit.
>
> At last the spangled Wednesfield bird,
> Began to show defeat,
> When Billy Lane he up and swore,
> The bird shouldn't be beat.
>
> For he would fight the biggest mon
> That came from Wil'n'all town,

When on the word old 'Cheeky Ned'
Got up and knocked him down.

To fight they went like bull-dogs,
As it is very well known,
Till 'Cheeky Ned' seized Billy's Thumb,
And bit it to the bone.

At this the Wednesfield men begun,
Their comrade's part to take,
And never was a fiercer fight
Fought at a village wake.

They beat the men from Wil'n'all town
Back to their town again,
And long they will remember,
This Wednesfield wake and main.

An interesting account of cocking is given in the columns of a local newspaper of the late nineteenth century. The writer recalls a number of stories about the game. One was concerned with hiring the Dudley Devil, a local wiseman, to recover a stolen cockerel:

In the glorious good old days when cruel sports were not prohibited ... there were very few public houses in the Black Country towns that were considered perfect without their cock-pits, and the greater part of the inhabitants thereof were enthusiastic cock-fighters, and did not scruple in the least to match their favourite birds in deadly combat against those of their surrounding neighbours. When 'a main' or a single battle was arranged between the representatives of two towns, the eventful day was looked forward to with the keenest interest, and was always marked as a great holiday, and some very curious means were adopted to raise the cash wherewith to back their respective favourites. It was often that people sold their fat pigs, their kits of pigeons, pledged their clothes, and even stripped their houses of the greater part of the furniture; in fact, they would sell or pawn anything they could lay their hands on for the above purpose. There was once, a good number of years ago, a great cock-fight arranged to take place between the fraternity of the towns of Willenhall and Wednesfield, and one of the enthusiastic admirers of the Wednesfield bird, 'Old Stamp' ... was rather hard-up at the time for the needful, and was puzzled for some time how to raise the wind, but at length he just bethought himself he had a good crop of potatoes on some ground he rented. He sought the aid of a friend for the loan of a few pounds on the growing crop with which he backed his favourite bird, but the Wednesfield chanticleer having lost the battle, 'Old Stamp' was never afterwards able to redeem his tubers, a circumstance with which he was taunted as he went about the district to the end of his days. Often these cruel encounters were the cause of bitter strife springing up between the respective partisans, and many severe battles were the result between the human bipeds after the close of the struggle between the feathered crowers. There were times when the two towns would club together for providing and training a number of cocks in order to give some neighbouring town a sound thrashing. On more than one occasion Willenhall and Wednesfield have thus become allies and pitted the best birds of each place against the pick of Wednesbury, Darlaston, or any other town for miles around, the combination in a general way proving victorious. A rather amusing occurrence in connection with cock-fighting came under my own observation nearly forty years ago, the hero of which was composed of a queer combination of the abilities characteristic of the old Black Country fogies of the olden time. This gentleman was known far and wide as "Old Boxer". He was a disciple of St. Crispin, and he had a lingering fondness for cock-fighting long after it was prohibited by the laws of the land, and on the occasion referred to he purchased a grand game-cock and turned it down among his neighbour's fowls. He was greatly delighted to witness the slaughter of the mongrel cocks by his through-bred bird, but his glee turned to sorrow one day when he made the discovery that his champion chanticleer had been spirited away by some unknown means. He was sadly put out over his loss, and the same day he hied him off to Dudley and sought the aid of the 'Dudley Devil', or 'Devil Dunn' as he was sometimes called, to find the culprit. His satanic majesty, after receiving his fee, promised to find out the thief and cause the stolen bird to be brought back in the course of a day or two, but his spells and charms were utterly useless in this case, and the ringing notes of that warlike rooster were no more heard in that neighbourhood. There are few people of mature years living in the Black Country at the present time, who have not heard ... something of the 'Wednesbury Cocking', and how, when the old stage-coach used to run through the town, one of the guards of those ancient vehicles was in the habit of playing on his bugle the air of a disreputable song composed to commemorate that battle.

Bull-baiting was another popular Staffordshire sport widely recorded in song and story. It was much simpler and cruder than cock-fighting, and seems to have been governed by few rules and regulations. It has been suggested that John of Gaunt was responsible for introducing it to England, for it is believed that it derived from bull-running, which he instituted at Tutbury, Staffordshire. Others suggest the sport originated because the Lord of Stamford, Earl Warren, leased part of his acreage to the local butchers on condition they supplied a bull to be baited by dogs each November. In the version of the sport, popular until it was banned in 1835, the bull was attached to a chain, which was fixed to a stake, and the 'bullot' would charge a few pence for each dog to run at the bull and pin it by the nose. The onlookers generally placed bets on the dog they thought likely to pin the bull either fastest or first. At Stone, in North Staffordshire, baiting was once a regular wake feature. W. Wells Bladen, describes it in his *Notes on the Folklore of Stone:*

> Bull and bear-baiting, and dog and cock-fighting, were some of the chief wakes attractions for the visitors who flocked into the town. Bears were baited behind the Unicorn Hotel ... Bulls in Granville-square, ... on the spot on which the Market Hall now stands, ... Baiting took place three times a-day, a small entrance fee being paid for each dog, the owner of the one which held the bull or the bear for the longest period receiving the prize – usually a leg of mutton or a copper kettle. The man in charge of the bull was called 'belot'. The last bull-baiting took place about 1830, where the railway-crossing now is, its tongue being torn out; ....

The sport was a cruel and bloody business, both baiters and baited frequently being maimed or killed. Most of the bull-baiting songs stress this aspect of the baits in graphic descriptions and rough and ready language. But one song, *The Bloxwich Wake,* stands out. It describes the strange events that took place during the wake of 1779:

> Come friends an' listen to my song,
> You shall not find it dulle,
> It is the strange and merry lay
> About ye Bloxwich bull.
>
> It was the wake of 'seventy nine,
> The village green was full,
> They said no towne afar or near
> Could boast so fine a bull.
>
> Ye dogs were brought, ye stakes were driven,
> And then there came a lull,
> While three tall men went oe'r the green
> To fetch ye famous bull.
>
> Now when they reached ye stable doore,
> Long faces did they pull,
> For lo! some knave had been afore
> An' taken away ye bull.
>
> Ye three tall men were sore afraid
> Their hearts wi' grief were full
> 'Gie us an howeres space,' they said,
> 'And we will find ye bull.'
>
> They searched from noon till twilight grey·
> An' then to evening dull,
> But never more ye people spied
> Ye tall men or ye bull.

Like many urban ballads of South Staffordshire, this one was directed to be sung to the tune called *The Wedgebury Cocking;* although many versions of the Wedgebury Cocking are known, the tune has not, as yet, been found. One of the best descriptions of a bull-baiting and its aftermath – a headlong flight through the streets – comes from a late nineteenth-century newspaper describing the events of a Bilston baiting, held some fifty or sixty years previously:

The dogs were at length let loose and began to cruelly torment the poor bull, which soon worked itself into a mad state of fury, and several of the canine fraternity were tossed high into the air, and descended among the vast crowd with sides torn open, and entrails protruding, as they fell heavily on the heads of the people. This state of things was carried on till the afternoon when the bull, frightfully worried about the head and nostrils, made a last mightly effort to free himself from his bondage. To the great consternation of all around the fastenings gave way, and the bull charged furiously among the crowd, upsetting scores in his mad rush for liberty. Thousands who seemed brave enough when the bull was safely chained, now took to their heels in all directions, but the infuriated beast in his mad gallop took a course up the main street. At that period the markets and fairs were held in that street, and being the wake time the thoroughfare was packed with people, and stalls of all descriptions lined the street on each side. These were soon deserted by their owners, who fled for safety in a great state of terror. The stalls were overturned by the mad rushes of the bull, the contents of one being mixed with those of another, all being scattered in hopeless ruin and confusion about the street and in the gutters. I believe a great many persons were badly injured by the falling stalls, and in coming in contact with his bullship, in their mad haste to make tracks for a safer quarter. But still the infuriated animal kept on his wild chase, dashing up and down the street, lashing his sides with his tail, snorting and bellowing in a frightful manner.

At length a band of pursuers formed themselves, armed with various weapons, and gave chase to the fugitive, but he defied all their efforts to recapture him for some hours, and eventually succeeded in getting out of the town, where he was shot later in the evening. The next day the carcase was dressed and cut up, and sold to the poor at twopence per pound. I had this description from an eye-witness of the affair, a good many years ago now – a maternal aunt of mine who was born in the year 1797, and was a young woman at the time of the occurrence.

Other sports of a similar nature, such as bear-baiting, dog-fighting and badger-drawing have produced little in the way of song or story, though they were popular in their time. Others, like boxing and wrestling, have been the subject of various songs and are similar in style to the sporting ballads included in this collection.

Apart from these organised sports, there were other more spontaneous pastimes. Most of them were small-scale affairs which took place annually or seasonally. Some, like whippet-racing and pigeon-flying, are still favourites at the present time.

Many were preserved in the leisure activities of children and young people. The game of French and English was still common all over Staffordshire in the 1860s. Two leaders were chosen, who in turn each elected ten followers. The stronger boys were mounted by the lighter ones and, on a signal from the umpire, the two teams ran at each other, in an effort to unseat the riders. Failing immediate success, the opponents came together in a hand-to-hand struggle to unhorse the riders. The battle went on until one team had won, or the umpire called the game to a halt and made his award. I remember playing this game at St Andrews Primary School, Wolverhampton, in 1948, though we did not call it French and English; it is still played in local school-playgrounds.

A most unusual, possibly unique custom, used to be the prerogative of teenagers in certain Black Country towns. Lawley describes it in his *Staffordshire Customs:*

Another local custom which survived to within the last 30 years was that of juvenile street fighting, that is to say the boys and young men in one street were in the habit of pitching themselves in mimic warfare against those of a neighbouring street. The combatants met by mutual consent at some given spot, and after various passages of verbal warfare, champions were selected to fight for the honour of their respective streets. Sometimes as many as three or four pitched battles thus occurred in one night, and if the victory was indecisive it frequently happened that the whole of the opponents took the matter up and began fighting with sticks, stones, and whatever weapons were handy. Then the weaker party had to seek safety in flight, pursued by the victors. The defeated party beat up their friends on the following night, and the same kind of hostilities again took place, ending by the flight of the weaker. These street fights used to last for several weeks, and often ended in serious injuries ... The custom was not confined to Wolverhampton but was common in most of our

Black Country towns. This mimic warfare we ourselves remember frequently occuring in Bilston thirty-two years ago, and a friend of ours carries the scar caused by a stone thrown during one of these encounters as he was passing the spot where the rival parties were encountering.

An interesting variation on village street-football used to take place from time to time at Bilston. The amusement was current in the seventeenth century, and lasted until the mid-nineteenth. On receiving news of a big military victory, the villagers made footballs or fireballs of hemp and flax, which were bound with strong twine and soaked in tar, or similar inflammable material. They were then put away until it was time for the game. A large bonfire was made on the Church Street side of Broadway, as it was then, and it was lit in the evening, when the crowds gathered to the ringing of the bells. Those who wished to play formed two teams 'without regard for numbers'; the first fireball was lit and thrown into a cleared space, while the onlookers cheered and shouted. The players kicked the ball to and fro, and burning pieces would fly into the crowd, who threw them back into the central area. At other times ladders were used to fetch the ball from the tops of houses. The spent fireballs found their way on to the bonfire and fresh supplies were lit. When all the balls had been used and the bonfire lay smouldering, crowd and players made their way home, leaving the constable of the watch to extinguish the embers of the fire. The game was last played at the news of the Battle of Alma, when many thousands gathered to take part. The newly-established police tried to prevent it taking place, but without success. The custom was eventually prohibited by the Board of Commissioners, appointed under the Bilston Improvement Act of 1850, who declared that it was too dangerous.

Staffordshire schoolboys once played a game similar to that known as nine men's morris. In the local variant the two opponents selected a piece of turf, on which they marked out a square by cutting a trench. The square, usually about a foot across, was divided in two, and both players took it in turn to throw a pen-knife into their half. The depth of entry was measured and the thrower allowed to cut away a corresponding width from his rectangle. The first to cut away all the turf was the winner. The Staffordshire version of nine men's morris was called 'Tit, tat, tow, all in a row' and was played by two players on a board marked into nine squares. Moves with counters were taken by turn, the aim being to prevent your opponent from getting his three counters in one line.

Prison Bars, widely-played game in the County, was also a popular spectator sport until well into the nineteenth century. Two matches held at Newcastle-under-Lyme in 1755 between Staffordshire and Cheshire 'drew together several Thousands of People of both Sexes and all ages'. In his *Staffordshire Folklore* Lawley describes the county version of the game in detail:

An equal number of players having been chosen on each side, two large areas were formed side by side, the boundaries being outlined by means of chalk or paint. In front of these bases, or "dens" – as they were known in Staffordshire – at a distance of twenty or thirty yards, a stake or stone was placed, to which the players had to run and touch before they could attempt to return to their home. The boundaries being finished, the players stood on the front line of the two dens, prepared the moment a rival player started to run to the boundary post to follow after and take him prisoner. The proceedings were something like this: The parties having 'tossed' for precedence, a player belonging to the side which had won the toss suddenly dashed out from his den, and with the utmost speed rushed to the boundary, which he had to touch, and then dart home again. A rival player started after him the moment the first one began to run, and if he succeeded in catching his opponent before he reached home, he took him prisoner and the latter was then unable to take further part until that game was over. While the first pair of players were running a second player from the first den seized an opportunity while the attention was arrested by the first runners to rush for the boundary and he was followed by a rival, as before. This was kept up until sometimes only one player remained in each den to protect it from being captured. Each pursuer could only follow the player he first followed. Sometimes more than one player started at the same moment to pursue a rival, in which case one of them had to return to his 'den', and if one of the opposite party rushed out and touched him before he could cross the line back again, he was taken prisoner. When the game had proceeded until nearly all were taken prisoners on one side, it was terminated by the capture of the den, while the few remaining players were running; for it was a rule of the game that when one side was hopelessly beaten the den-keeper must make a run for the boundary like the other players, and in his absence the den was taken, and the game ended with cries of "Burn the den, burn the den."

Fewer players were required for Tip the Cat or Tip Cat, which was still popular in the late nineteenth century. The cat was a double-shaped piece of wood, about six inches long. The player stood at the centre of a large circle and struck the cat with a club. The cat then rose into the air in a circular motion, and the player attempted to hit it out of the circle. If he failed, another player took his place. Following a successful hit, the player would call out a number to be counted as his score. The distance from the boundary of the ring to the cat was then measured with the club, and if the number called by the player exceeded the measurement, the player was out; if not the number was added to his score.

Two more games that were popular until the mid-nineteenth century were Dog Stick and Dog in the Hole; both seem to have lost favour by the end of the century. Dog stick was played with a hard wooden ball, sometimes known as a 'knurr'. The ball was struck with a club, and the player who sent it the greatest distance in a given number of strokes was the winner. Dog in the Hole was a more complicated game. It was played by four players, two either side. Two holes about six feet apart were dug in the ground and a player holding a club or cudgel stood by each hole. The other two players stood behind their opponents and, in turn, they would throw a tip cat to the player at the opposite end. He struck the cat as far as possible; while the opposite side ran for the cat, the two club holders alternately struck their clubs together, then dipped the points in the holes; this was known as 'dogging the hole'. If they could reach the count of five before their opponents retrieved the cat and threw it in the hole, they took another turn. On this second strike the players were obliged to exchange 'dogs' three times, and between each exchange they had to 'dog the hole' with the end of their clubs. If the cat was retrieved and placed in the hole before the completion of the sequence, the game was brought to an end. If the cat was placed in the hole before the club holders could complete 'dogging the hole' after the first strike, then the two fielders took their turn with the clubs.

A ball was also used for a game of divination. The ball was tossed in the air, while the thrower clapped his hands as many times as possible before having to catch the ball. The number of claps represented the number of years he would have to live. There are various games popular in eighteenth and nineteenth centuries that are still current. Rounders and tutball, a game like rounders, but using the hand for a bat, are played as spontaneous children's games and as organised play-ground games. 'Cuckoo', or hide and seek is very widely played. In the version called 'cuckoo' one of those in hiding would call this out when all were hidden. The nineteenth-century game known as 'Stag Warning' is still a popular play-ground game, though it is not known by this name and the traditional rhymes are no longer chanted. The boy selected as the 'stag' chases the other players and, when he has ticked one, the two join hands and attempt to catch the others. As each person is ticked, so he joins the line; the two children at the end of the line tick the runners with their free hands and the body of the line is used to 'round up' the free runners. The last free runner becomes the new 'stag' and in the nineteenth-century game he would have called out:

> Stag-warning, stag warning,
> Come out tomorrow morning.

or, alternatively,

> Stig, Stag, a rumping, rumping stag,
> The first one as I catch I'll put him in a bag.

At the end of a long summer day of game-playing the popular nineteenth-century cry to end the session ran:

> The game's broke up,
> The shop's shut up
> Ready for tomorrow morning!

Notes

1 *Ghosts and Graves* (pages 15-26)

BLACK MERE OF MORRIDGE: Dr R. Plot, *The Natural History of Staffordshire*, 1686, 2-24 (all references to Plot are to chapter and section); Book 5, *Newspaper Cuttings*, undated, note XLV, 33, West Bromwich Library.

JACK O' LANTERN OR WILL O' THE WISP: W. Wells Bladen, 'Notes on the Folklore of North Staffordshire, chiefly collected at Stone', *North Staffordshire Field Club Transactions*, Vol. XXXV, 1899-1901, 135; G. T. Lawley, *Staffordshire Customs, Superstitions and Folklore*, Collection of Newspaper Articles, undated, written and compiled by G. T. Lawley, c. 1922, Bilston Library.

HEADLESS HORSEMAN OF THE MOORLANDS: *The Staffordshire Sentinel*, Summer Number, 1909, 55, extracted from a paper by Henry Wedgwood, *Up and Down the County*. Vol. 2, 1881, 33-48.

THE KIDSGROVE BOGGART: W. Wells Bladen, 144; tale extracted from W. Wells Bladen paper and printed in *The Staffordshire Sentinel*, Summer Number, 1910, 18.

WHITE RABBIT OF ETRURIA: H. A. Wedgwood, *People of the Potteries*, 1970, 21-4; H. A. Wedgwood, *The Romance of Staffordshire*, Vol. 1, 1877-9, 45-50; H. A. Wedgwood, *Up and Down the County*, Vol. 2, 1881, 33-48, contains details of the murder; G. T. Lawley, 38.

MAN-MONKEY: C. S. Burne, edited with additions from the collections of G. F. K. Jackson, *Shropshire Folklore*, 1883, 106.

CORNHILL CROSS GHOST; SPOT LANE BOGGART; HEADLESS WHITE DOG; ECCLESHALL ROAD GREYHOUND: W. Wells Bladen, 147, 146, 147, 142, respectively.

HAND OF GLORY AND GHOST AT WHITE HART INN: *Walsall Observer*, 5.3.57; Personal letter, 1.11.71, from F. N. Bowler, Borough Librarian, Walsall; information on the Hand of Glory, E. and M. A. Radford, *Encyclopedia of Superstitions*, 1948, 1961, 179.

QUEENS HOTEL GHOST: *Express and Star*, 24.12.74; 36.

COACH AND HORSES GHOST: *Express and Star*, 27.4.76, 22.

GHOST AT FACTORY OF W. T. COPELAND: *Evening Sentinel*, 8.3.67.

GHOSTS OF NORBURY MANOR: C. S. Burne, 50, 51.

GHOST OF HADEN HALL: J. Wilson Jones, *The History of the Black Country*, undated, circa 1955, 104.

GHOST OF HULTON VALE: *The Staffordshire Sentinel*, 11.

CURFEW BELL GHOST: F. W. Hackwood, *A Staffordshire Miscellany*, 1927, 52.

MISER OF OULTON VICARAGE: W. Wells Bladen, 143.

BILSTON BUTCHER'S GHOST: G. T. Lawley, 39.

RUSHTON GHOST: W. Wells Bladen, 144; *The Staffordshire Sentinel*, 18;

SPRING HEEL JACK: Stories still in general circulation; G. T. Lawley, 39.

MOLLY LEE: C. S. Burne, 120; G. T. Lawley, 38.

COMBERFORD DEATH WARNING: Dr R. Plot, 8-107; G. T. Lawley, 38.

BLACK DOG AS DEATH WARNING: F. W. Hackwood, *Sedgley Researches* 1898, 106.

WHITE RABBIT AT KIDSGROVE: W. Wells Bladen, 144; Peter Travis, *In Search of the Supernatural*, 1975, 71-73, contains various stories and sightings from Staffordshire.

COLLIER'S GHOST: G. T. Lawley, 4.

WHITE RABBIT OF BILSTON: G. T. Lawley, 5.

CUTTING A TURF: C. H. Poole, *The Customs, Superstitions and Legends of the County of Stafford* undated, circa 1875, 75, 76; F. W. Hackwood, 64.

BRADNOP GHOST; HILDERSTONE MANOR POLTERGEIST: W. Wells Bladen, 145, 146.

RAW HEAD AND BLOODY BONES: BILSTON BROOK HAUNTING: G. T. Lawley, 39, 38.

CACCHIONE FAMILY GHOSTS: Personal communication from Joseph Cacchione, Wolverhampton, 1974.

2 *Legendary Tales* (pages 27-33)

LEGEND OF LICHFIELD OR MARTYRDOM OF ST AMPHIBALOUS: S. Shaw, *The History and Antiquities of Staffordshire,* Vol. 1, 1798, 231-2; Dr R. Plot, *The Natural History of Staffordshire,* 1684, 10-12; C. H. Poole, *The Customs, Superstitions and Legends of the County of Stafford,* undated, 102; Book 5, *Newspaper Cuttings,* undated, item XXXIII, 42, West Bromwich Library; M. and J. Raven, *Folklore of the Black Country,* Vol. 2, 1966, 59; F. Grice, *Folk Tales of the West Midlands,* 1952, 137-40, including the verse 'Three Slain Kings'.

WULFAD: C. H. Poole, 109-14.

ST KENELM: Dr R. Plot, 10-32; C. H. Poole, 93-5; S. Shaw, 241-2.

PANTHER OF GIFFARD'S CROSS: F. W. Hackwood, *Staffordshire Stories,* 1906, 11-14; C. H. Poole, 98; J. Timbs and A. Gunn, *Abbeys and Castles of England and Wales,* Vol. 2, 1924, 555, 556; M. and J. Raven, 23; Vol. 3, *Newspaper Cuttings,* undated, item 935, 25, West Bromwich Library; Book 5, *Newspaper Cuttings,* undated, item XCIII, 62, West Bromwich Library; Mottled Brown Covered Volume, article 'Bits of the Old Black Country', by Alfred Camden Pratt, extracted from the *Midland Counties Express,* 29.3.84, 113, Wolverhampton Library; Thin black-covered volume, 1st page an etching of Tong Church, undated, 174, Wolverhampton Library; F. Grice, *Folk Tales of the West Midlands,* 1952, 125-9.

WEEFORD STONES: C. H. Poole, 123, 124.

WANDERING JEW: C. H. Poole, 104-6; Rev. F. Bright, *The Tale of Ipstones,* 1937, 162, 163.

HERMIT OF CANNOCK CHASE: J. P. Jones, *Staffordshire Collections*, 1883, 190-2, Newspaper Cutting, 'Bits of the Old Black Country', by Alfred Camden Pratt and sub titled 'The Hermit and the Hare', from the *Midland Counties Express*, 22.12.82; An article in the AA publication *No Through Road* gives a similar story, but the hermit is called Dick Slee, and he left home because of a nagging wife.

GYPSY WOMAN IN TETTENHALL CHURCH: Story of general currency in Tettenhall. P. Raven, personal communication, 1976.

3   *The Devil, Witches, Dragons, Giants and Fairies* (pages 34-48)

DEVIL AND BLACKBERRIES: C. H. Poole, *The Customs, Superstitions and Legends of the County of Stafford*, undated, 85.

'AT KYDDEMOOR GREEN': F. W. Hackwood, *Staffordshire Customs, Superstitions and Folklore*, 1924, 166.

'AUDLEY', ETC: F. W. Hackwood, 166.

'WHEN SATAN STOOD' F. W. Hackwood, 166; D. R. Guttery, *Pensnett and Kingswindford*, 1950, 32.

'HE STAGGERED ON': D. R. Guttery, 32.

'THE DEVIL STOOD'; 'THE DEVIL RAN'; 'STANTON ON THE STONES': F. W. Hackwood, 166-7.

FAIRY RINGS WHERE DEVILS DANCE: Dr R. Plot, *The Natural History of Staffordshire, 1684*, 1-24.

WITCHES AT MIDSUMMER PARLIAMENT; DRAWING MOON DOWN; BLOOD RED MOON: G. T. Lawley, *Staffordshire Customs, Superstitions and Folklore*, undated, 94A, Collection of Newspaper Articles, Bilston Library.

SUN WHEELS AND WYRLEY BONK RHYME, CARRYING BURNING TORCHES: G. T. Lawley, 107.

RULES TO UNCOVER WITCH: G. T. Lawley, 19.

WITCH OF GETTLIFFE'S YARD: M. A. Miller, *Olde Leeke*, Vol. 11, 1900, 113-4.

WITCH AS WHITE RABBIT: F. W. Hackwood, *Sedgley Researches*, 1905, 107.

'FIXING' A VICTIM: W. Wells Bladen, 'Notes on the Folklore of North Staffordshire Chiefly Collected at Stone', in *North Staffordshire Field Club Transactions*, Vol. XXXV, 1899-1901, 147-8.

TRIAL OF RICHARD BATE: G. T. Lawley, 19A; F. W. Hackwood, 153-5.

STICKING A BULLOCK'S HEART: F. W. Hackwood, 155.

EXORCIST AT FARM; POWDER ON SHOVEL: G. T. Lawley, 19A.

TRANSFORMING A BAG OF FLOUR: C. S. Burne, *Shropshire Folklore*, 1883, 159.

WITCH BROOCHES: F. W. Hackwood, 155.

'ST JOHN'S WORT': G. T. Lawley, 19A.

DRAWING BLOOD OF WITCH IN HUMAN FORM: G. T. Lawley, 19A; W. Wells Bladen, 149.

DRAWING BLOOD OF WITCH IN ANIMAL FORM: G. T. Lawley, 86A.

THROW OBJECT TO DRAW BLOOD: G. T. Lawley, 19/19A.

THIGH BONES, ROPE FROM HANGED MURDERER: G. T. Lawley, 19.

UNBROKEN EGG SHELL HALVES: F. W. Hackwood, *Religious Wednesbury*, 1900, 127.

WISE WOMAN AT LEEK: W. Wells Bladen, 148.

OUD ELIJER COTTON, A WISE MAN: W. Wells Bladen, 148.

CHURCHWARDENS CONSULT WISE MAN: C. H. Poole, 72-3; F. W. Hackwood, 153; G. T. Lawley, 19A.

DEVIN DUNN: F. W. Hackwood, *Staffordshire Customs, Superstitions and Folklore*, 1924, 155-6; Newspaper Cutting, Number 2,308, *Local Notes and Queries*, item 1973, found pasted in C. F. G. Clarke's *Curiosities of the Black Country*, contributed by John Rowley, research assistant at Wolverhampton Polytechnic, 1973.

WISE MAN FROM SEDGLEY: G. T. Lawley, 19A; C. H. Poole, 72/73; F. W. Hackwood, 153.

WISE MAN FROM HELL LANE; BIBLE AND FRONT DOOR KEY: G. T. Lawley, 19A.

WHITE WITCHES AT WALSALL: *Express and Star*, 26.8.76.

'THE DRAGON OF WEDGEBURY': F. W. Hackwood, *Olden Wednesbury*, 1899, 33.

STAKE DRIVEN THROUGH GIANT: W. Wells Bladen, 148.

HOLY AUSTIN ROCK: F. W. Hackwood, *Staffordshire Stories*, 1906, 77.

FAIRIES CHANGING SITE OF WALSALL AND HANCHURCH CHURCHES: C. H. Poole, 75.

PUCK, LOB, ROBIN GOODFELLOW: G. T. Lawley, 91A.

GOOD FAIRIES: G. T. Lawley, 91A/93.

FAIRY RINGS: Dr R. Plot, 1-17, 37.

REWARD TO HUMANS: G. T. Lawley, 93.

TAKING A CHILD AND LEAVING FAIRY: G. T. Lawley, 93; Rev. F. Bright, *The Tale of Ipstones,* 1937, 172.

CHRISTEN CHILD FOR PROTECTION: G. T. Lawley, 93.

LEAVE CAKE FOR FAIRIES: FAIRIES REPAIR PLOUGH: Rev. F. Bright, 172.

HOB AND NOB; BEN CROWDER AND THE IMPS; UGLY DWARF AND THE PIT EXPLOSION: G. T. Lawley, 91.

DICK THE DEVIL AND THE EVIL IMPS: G. T. Lawley 91/91A.

4   Healing Charms and Magic Cures (pages 49-54)

WISE WOMAN AT THE HEN AND CHICKENS: C. H. Poole, *The Customs, Superstitions and Legends of the County of Stafford, undated, 83.*

TOOTHACHE A PAIN FROM THE DEVIL: C. S. Burne, *Shropshire Folklore,* 1883, 191-2.

PETER . . . SAT, ETC: F. W. Hackwood, *Staffordshire Customs, Superstitions and Folklore,* 1924, 156; W. Wells Bladen, 'Notes on the Folklore of North Staffordshire Chiefly Collected at Stone', *North Staffordshire Field Club Transactions,* XXXV, 1899-1901, 150.

CRUSH LADYBIRD: F. W. Hackwood, 156.

DEAD MAN'S TOOTH: F. W. Hackwood, 150; C. H. Poole, 83; Book 5, *Newspaper Cuttings,* Note LVII, undated, 41, West Bromwich Library.

BONE SHEEP'S HEAD: *The Staffordshire Sentinel* (Newspaper), Summer Number, 1909, 57; C. H. Poole, 83.

MOLE'S FEET: C. H. Poole, 83; W. Wells Bladen, 149.

WHOOPING COUGH, LORD'S PRAYER: Rev. E. Deacon, 'Some Quaint Customs and Superstitions in North Staffordshire and Elsewhere', *North Staffordshire Field Club Transactions,* Vol. LXIV, 1929, 20-1.

MOUSE FRIED IN BUTTER: Rev. E. Deacon, 21.

MOUSE EAR PLANT: F. W. Hackwood, 150.

NEW MOON RHYME: Rev. E. Deacon, 21; C. H. Poole, 82.

BRAMBLE BUSH: F. W. Hackwood, 150; C. H. Poole, 82.

FEET OF TOAD: F. W. Hackwood, 150.

RABBIT FOR CURING CHIN COUGH: C. H. Poole, 82.

HARE'S FOOT: C. H. Poole, 82.

HAIR FROM DONKEY; CHIN COUGH: C. H. Poole, 83; Rev. E. Deacon, 21; W. Wells Bladen, 148, passing three times under the belly of a donkey and giving a child milk to drink from a saucer from which a rabbit has lapped, also quoted by Bladen, 148, 149.

HAIR FROM DONKEY; MEASLES: Rev. E. Deacon, 21.

PEPPERCORN NECKLACE: C. H. Poole, 83.

FITS, MOLE'S FOOT CHARM; TIP OF A BEAST'S TONGUE FOR TOOTHACHE: W. Wells Bladen, 149.

CHARM WARTS WITH HAND OF HANGED CRIMINAL OR DEAD MAN'S HAND: Rev. E. Deacon, 24; Summer Sentinel, 57, Book 5, 41; C. H. Poole, 84.

WART CHARMERS PASSING HANDS OVER WARTS: Rev. E. Deacon, 24.

CHARM WARTS WITH WHEAT GRAINS: W. Wells Bladen, 149.

RUB WART WITH STOLEN BEEF: W. Wells Bladen, 149; C. H. Poole, 84; Book 8, *Newspaper Cuttings,* undated, no. 2402, 80, West Bromwich Library.

RUB WART WITH BEEF AND THEN HANG ON THORN: W. Wells Bladen, 149; C. H. Poole also mentions the same technique using a black snail, 84.

RUB WART WITH ONION; BLOW ON WART AT NEW MOON; DIP WARTS IN PIG'S BLOOD: W. Wells Bladen, 149.

RUB WARTS WITH TAIL OF TORTOISE SHELL TOM CAT: C. H. Poole, 84; Rev. E. Deacon, 23.

WEDDING RING TO CURE POWKE OR STYE: F. W. Hackwood, 152; *Staffordshire Sentinel,* 57.

ROUNDING FOR SPLINTERS: C. S. Burne, 185.

POTATO TO WARD OFF RHEUMATISM: *Staffordshire Sentinel,* 57; C. H. Poole, 83; W. Wells Bladen, 149.

MAGNET TO CURE RHEUMATISM: C. H. Poole, 83.

CURE CRAMP DRAWING ON STOCKING: W. Wells Bladen, 150.

CURE CRAMP WITH RHYME: F. W. Hackwood, 152.

CURE MUMPS WALKING ROUND STREAM, ETC.: C. H. Poole, 84.

CHILBLAINS BEATEN WITH HOLLY: C. H. Poole, 83.

BLOOD FROM BLACK CAT'S TAIL: Rev. E. Deacon, 24.

EAGLESTONE: F. W. Hackwood, 151.

MISTLETOE: G. T. Lawley, *Staffordshire Customs, and Folklore,* undated, 43A, *A Collection of Newspaper Articles,* Bilston Library.

CHOKE DAMP CURED BY EARTH: C. H. Poole, 82.

ROYAL TOUCH: F. W. Hackwood, 151; C. H. Poole, 84.

CURING CATTLE DISEASE WITH TURF: F. W. Hackwood, 156; Dr Robert Plot, *The Natural History of Staffordshire,* 1686, 9-96.

'SHREW ASH': F. W. Hackwood, 156; Dr Robert Plot, 6-51.
CURE CROUP WITH PIGEON: F. W. Hackwood, 150.
CURE BY SYMPATHY: W. Wells Bladen, 150.

5   *Cradle to Grave* (pages 55-75)

WEIGHING NEW BORN CHILD: F. W. Hackwood, *Staffordshire Customs, Superstitions and Folklore,* 1924, 57; W. Wells Bladen, 'Notes on the Folklore of North Staffordshire chiefly collected at Stone', *North Staffordshire Field Club Transactions,* Vol. XXXV, 1899-1901, 154.

CARRYING BABY UPSTAIRS: F. W. Hackwood, 154; W. Wells Bladen, 154.

CUTTING NAILS OR HAIR BEFORE TWELVE MONTHS: F. W. Hackwood, 57; W. Wells Bladen, 154, nor look in a looking-glass; C. H. Poole, *The Customs, Superstitions and Legends of the County of Stafford,* undated, 85.

WASHING PALMS OF INFANT: C. H. Poole, 85.

CATS SUCKING BREATH; MOTHER CHURCHED BEFORE VISITING: F. W. Hackwood, 57.

ROCKING EMPTY CRADLE: F. W. Hackwood, 57; C. H. Poole, 85.

CHILD BORN WITH CAUL: F. W. Hackwood, 57.

FIRST TEETH BURNED; BORN ON FRIDAY; THE WENCH THEY CHRISTENED BEN: W. Wells Bladen, 154; *Poems of Lye Waste,* by *A Cradley Bagpudden,* an undated booklet printed by Hemming of Stourbridge (c. 1870).

ASH LEAF TO FIND HUSBAND'S NAME: C. S. Burne, *Shropshire Folklore,* 1883, 180.

APPLE PARING: F. W. Hackwood, 46.

MOON TO FIND HUSBAND'S NAME: G. T. Lawley, *Staffordshire Customs, Superstitions and Folklore,* undated, 94, *A Collection of Newspaper Articles,* Bilston Library.

WISE WOMEN TO REVEAL HUSBAND'S NAME; PAPER CHARMS TO ATTRACT LOVERS: Rev. F. Bright, *Tale of Ipstones,* 1937, 165; Vol. 6 *Newspaper Cuttings,* undated, 19, 20, Wednesbury Library.

BACHELORS' BUTTONS: Dr S. Jackson Coleman, *Treasury of Folklore, Staffordshire Folklore,* No. 44, Pamphlet, 1955.

TWELVE STONES: Rev. F. Bright, 165.

DRAGON'S BLOOD AND FLANNEL: Dr S. Jackson Coleman.

SPRIG OF EVERGREEN: C. H. Poole, 74.

THREAD HAIR THROUGH FINGER RING: Dr S. Jackson Coleman.

HAIR AS BAD LUCK: W. Wells Bladen, 155.

SONG, OF GIRL WANTING TO WED COLLIER: F. W. Hackwood, *Collections,* Wednesbury Library.

WOOD ANEMONE AT A WEDDING: Rev. E. Deacon, 'Some Quaint Customs and Superstitions in North Stafford and Elsewhere', *North Staffordshire Field Club Transactions,* Vol. LXIV, 1929, 26, Wood anemone associated with death in folk culture and sometimes known as 'Death Bloom'.

MARRY ON A FRIDAY OR IN MAY; GOOD LUCK FOR BRIDES: W. Wells Bladen, 155.

LOAF RISES HIGH AND TOPPLES OVER: C. S. Burne, 276;

COUPLE WITH BACKS TO HORSES: W. Wells Bladen, 155.

BRIDE AND GROOM NOT ACCOMPANIED BY FATHER OR MOTHER: F. W. Hackwood, *Staffordshire Customs, Superstitions and Folklore,* 1924, 61; F. W. Hackwood, *Religious Wednesbury,* 1900, 129.

BRIDE PRESENTED WITH WHITE GLOVES: F. W. Hackwood, *Staffordshire Customs, Superstitions and Folklore,* 1924, 61, white for purity.

FLOWERS AT WEDDINGS; PLAYING THE BRIDE TO CHURCH; ACCOMPANIED BY MOUNTED CAVALCADE: F. W. Hackwood, 61.

CHIMNEY SWEEP: Personal communication, Mrs K. Raven, Tettenhall, July 1976.

DIFFERENT GATES FOR WEDDINGS AND FUNERALS: W. Wells Bladen, 156.

SPORTS AND BRIDE BALL: F. W. Hackwood, 61.

SLIDING DOWN HAND-RAIL: Dr S. Jackson Coleman

BARRING WAY WITH ROPE: Rev. E. Deacon, 31.

WEDDING CAKE BENEATH PILLOW: W. Wells Bladen, 156.

CHASTITY LOST IF WEDDING RING REMOVED: F. W. Hackwood, 61.

LOST OR BROKEN WEDDING RINGS: F. W. Hackwood, 61.

SEVEN YEARS SEPARATION: W. Wells Bladen, 155.

WIFE-SELLING: F. W. Hackwood, 70-73; G. T. Lawley, 67, 67a, 68, 68a; F. W. Hackwood, *Sedgley Researches,* 1898, 108; F. W. Hackwood, *The Annals of Willenhall,* 1908, 187; M. A. Miller, *Olde Leeke,* Vol. 1, 1900, 177.

'HE DROVE HIS WIFE TO MARKET': G. T. Lawley, 67.

SONG, 'WIFE FOR SALE': G. T. Lawley, 68.

LEGAL DECISIONS AGAINST WIFE SELLING: Letter to author from the Assistant Librarian, Institute of Historical Research, November 1971.

ROUGH MUSIC AT TUTBURY: *The Weekly Sentinel,* Sentinel Summer Number, 1912, 18.

STRAW AT DOOR OF WIFE BEATERS; MARCHINGTON; SCOLDS; CANAL TRAFFIC SUSPENDED: G. T. Lawley, 66a.

WYCHNOR FLITCH: S. Shaw, *The History and Antiquities of Staffordshire,* Vol. 1, 1798, 120-21; S. Erdeswick, *A Survey of Staffordshire,* 1844, 321-22; R. K. Dent and J. Hill, *Historic Staffordshire,* 1896, 127; W. Beresford, *Memorials of Old Staffordshire,* 1909, 57-8; personal communication, Tamworth Borough Librarian, 1971; personal communication, Burton upon Trent Borough Librarian, 1971; personal communication, Owner of Wychnor Park, 1971; Dr R. Plot, *The Natural History of Staffordshire,* 1686, 10-77, 78, 79; F. W. Hackwood, 67-9; C. H. Poole, *The Customs, Superstitions and Legends of the County of Stafford,* undated, 53, 54.

CLEANING WINDOWS; EMPTY PURSE; NEW SHOES; UMBRELLA; PEACOCKS' FEATHERS: Mrs K. Raven

MAY BLOSSOM: Mrs K. Raven; Rev. E. Deacon, 26.

BREAKING A MIRROR: Mrs K. Raven; also general currency at present time; C. H. Poole, 79.

PASSING ON STAIRS: Mrs K. Raven.

KNIVES AND SCISSORS: Mrs K. Raven; W. Wells Bladen, 151.

KNIVES: Mrs K. Raven; W. Wells Bladen, 151.

THE MOON: Mrs K. Raven; G. T. Lawley, 94.

BLACK CAT: Mrs K. Raven; also general currency; C. H. Poole, 80.

WALKING UNDER A LADDER: Mrs K. Raven; also general currency; W. Wells Bladen, 151.

HORSE SHOES: Mrs K. Raven; also general currency.

SPILLING SALT: Mrs K. Raven; also general currency; C. H. Poole, 78; W. Wells Bladen, 151; F. W. Hackwood, 149.

DROPPED GLOVE: Mrs K. Raven.

FREE WISH: Mrs K. Raven, also general currency in case of four leaf clover.

JOURNEY ON FRIDAY: W. Wells Bladen, 151.

TURNING BACK OR SAYING GOODBYE AT GATE: W. Wells Bladen, 151; C. S. Burne, 274.

MEETING A WOMAN ON WAY TO WORK: F. W. Hackwood, 147; Amy Lyons, *Black Country Sketches,* 1901, 13.

TOUCH IRON: Rev. E. Deacon, 19.

MAGPIES: C. H. Poole, 80.

FROG: C. H. Poole, 86.

WOOD ANEMONE: Rev. E. Deacon, 26.

HAWTHORN HOUSE: C. S. Burne, 244.

CROOKED SIXPENCE: F. W. Hackwood, 148.

LOOKING AT NEW MOON: G. T. Lawley, 94; Mrs K. Raven.

TURNING A CHAIR: F. W. Hackwood, 149.

HAIRCUT: W. Wells Bladen, 153.

NUMBER THIRTEEN: W. Wells Bladen, 152; also in general currency at present. As recently as 9 July 1976 the *Express and Star* reported that a widow living in Wednesbury applied to have the number on her door changed from 13 to 12A, after a run of ill health and deaths in the family. The request was allowed by Sandwell technical services committee.

LUCKY ODD NUMBERS; THIRTEEN PEOPLE AT TABLE; DOUBLE NUT; MOLE ON LEFT ARM; NAIL CUTTING RHYME: W. Wells Bladen, 153, 151, 151, 153, 154, respectively.

ITCHING NOSE: F. W. Hackwood, 149.

ITCHY PALM: F. W. Hackwood, 148; W. Wells Bladen, 153.

FINGER NAILS; WHITE SPOT ON TONGUE: F. W. Hackwood, 149.

EARS BURNING: F. W. Hackwood, 149; C. H. Poole, 79; W. Wells Bladen, 153.

HAIRY MEN: F. W. Hackwood, 149.

THROWING HAIR ON FIRE; DRAWING HAIR THROUGH HAND: W. Wells Bladen, 153.

INVOLUNTARY SHUDDER: W. Wells Bladen, 153; C. H. Poole, 78; still in general currency.

MONEY SPIDER: F. W. Hackwood, 149.

SPRING LAMB; DREAMING OF THE DEAD; DREAMING OF CHILDREN; DREAMING OF INSECTS: W. Wells Bladen, 151, 152, 152, 152, respectively.

HORSE SHOE: W. Wells Bladen, 152; still in general currency.

KNIFE AND FORK: F. W. Hackwood, 149.

COALS: W. Wells Bladen, 151.

SOOT: F. W. Hackwood, 149; W. Wells Bladen, 151; C. H. Poole, 86.

PUDDING: C. H. Poole, 86.

TREES LOSING LEAVES: Rev. E. Deacon, 26.

SPIT ON FIRST MONEY: F. W. Hackwood, 148.

TURN MONEY AND SPIT ON IT: Book 8, *Newspaper Cuttings,* West Bromwich Library, undated, 80, no. 2402.

SPIT ON LEFT SHOE: F. W. Hackwood, 147; C. H. Poole, 81.

BREAK BAD LUCK AT CARDS: Vol. 6, *Newspaper Cuttings,* 19-20.

PIN RHYMES: W. Wells Bladen, 152.

PERMANENT HEADACHE: C. H. Poole, 85.

BURNING FERN: F. W. Hackwood, 149; G. T. Lawley, 7A; C. H. Poole, 85.

COCKS AND ROBINS: Vol. 6, *Newspaper Cuttings,* 19-20.

CATCHING WAGTAIL: C. H. Poole, 80.

PIGS: W. Wells Bladen, 152.

SEEDS: W. Wells Bladen, 152.

HENS AND YOLK-LESS EGGS: W. Wells Bladen, 153.

CHARMS OF METAL: M. A. Miller, 299-300.

FAMILY CHARMS: M. A. Miller, 299.

LOGS BURNING BADLY: Rev. E. Deacon, 26.

SUN AND MOON; SLEEPING; MAN IN THE MOON: G. T. Lawley, 94, 94A, 94A, respectively.

RAVEN: C. H. Poole, 80.

MAGPIES; MIXING BRAN MASH: M. A. Miller, 300.

BLACK CALF: W. Wells Bladen, 156; F. W. Hackwood, 147; C. H. Poole, 77.

WHITE BIRD: W. Wells Bladen, 157.

ROBIN; COCKEREL; FRUIT TREES; GUTTERING OF FAT: W. Wells Bladen, 158.

BROOM OF MAY: Rev. E. Deacon, 28.

CLOCKS STOP: W. Wells Bladen, 158.

WARNING KNOCKS; MARBLES: F. W. Hackwood, 147.

DIAMOND CREASE IN NAPKIN; NAKED LIGHT OUT OF HOUSE: W. Wells Bladen, 158.

MOON RHYME, CLOT OF BLOOD: G. T. Lawley, 94A.

DREAM WARNING: F. W. Hackwood, 148; also in common currency in present day.

PILLOW MATTRESS: W. Wells Bladen, 156; C. H. Poole, 86.

COINS; SALT; WHITE SHEET; MEETING FUNERAL: W. Wells Bladen, 156.

RAIN AT FUNERAL: W. Wells Bladen, 156; personal communication, Mrs K. Raven, Tettenhall, July 1976.

SUNSHINE ON MOURNER: Mrs K. Raven.

NIGHT BURIAL FOR SUICIDES: W. Payne, *Stafford and its Associations*, 1887, 132.

RIGHT THUMB OF CORPSE: W. Wells Bladen, 158.

GREEN TURK: C. S. Burne, 240.

TOUCHING A DEAD BODY: W. Wells Bladen, 158; For death omens see also F. W. Hackwood, *Staffordshire Curiosities*, 1905, 42-8.

'COLD BLOWS THE WIND': R. Palmer, *Songs of the Midlands*, 1972, 29, from the singing of George Dunn, Quarry Bank, West Midlands, noted by Charles Parker in March 1971. George Dunn was 'discovered' by Rhoma Bowdler in 1970. His father and grandfather were Black Countrymen and he learned his songs from his father. Apart from his unusual tunes and singing style, George Dunn forms an important link in the Black Country traditional song chain, since his is the only proof, other than odd broadsides and collected snippets, that the Black Country once had a tradition of country songs. Also on LP record, Leader LEE 4042.

6 *The Turning Year* (pages 76-144)

January

FIRST FOOTING: Vol. 6, *Newspaper Cuttings*, undated, 30B, Article, 'New Year Customs in the Midlands', West Bromwich Library; W. Wells Bladen, 'Notes on The Folklore of North Staffordshire chiefly collected at Stone', in *North Staffordshire Field Club Transactions*, Vol. XXXV, 1899-1901, 159; Amy Lyons, *Black Country Sketches*, 1901, 4; E. A. Underhill, *The Story of the Ancient Manor of Sedgley*, 1941, 458.

'THE COCK SAT UP IN THE YEW TREE': Amy Lyons, 4; E. A. Underhill, 458.

OPENING DOOR BEFORE MIDNIGHT: Amy Lyons, 4.

WASSAIL BOWL: W. Wells Bladen, 159; Vol. 6, *Newspaper Cuttings*, 30B; G. T. Lawley, *Staffordshire Customs, Superstitions and Folklore*, undated, 45A/46, *A Collection of Newspaper Cuttings*, Bilston Library.

CLASHING OF HAMMERS ON IRONS: G. T. Lawley, 45A-46.

BANDAGED BELLS MUFFLED PEAL: Vol. 6, *Newspaper Cuttings*, 30B; G. T. Lawley, 45A-46.

BRIGHT PEAL OF BELLS; BONFIRES; GIVING FIRE, SACRED FIRE: G. T. Lawley, 45A-46.

COLLIERS REFUSING TO WORK: Vol. 6, *Newspaper Cuttings,* 30B; G. T. Lawley, 4.

JACK OF HILTON: Dr Robert Plot, *Natural History of Staffordshire,* 1686, 10-65; F. W. Hackwood, *Staffordshire Customs, Superstitions and Folklore,* 1924, 1-6; F. W. Hackwood, *Staffordshire Curiosities,* 1905, 99-102; Letter from R. L. Vernon, previous owner of Hilton Hall, November 1971, Author's MSS; Book 1, *Newspaper Cuttings,* item no. 4329, 34, West Bromwich Library; M. and J. Raven, *Folklore and Songs of the Black Country,* Vol. 3, 1967, 1-12.

ABBOTS BROMLEY HOBBY: Dr Robert Plot, 10-66; G. T. Lawley, 78/78A; F. W. Hackwood, *Staffordshire Customs, Superstitions and Folklore,* 1924, 5-6: Book 5, *Newspaper Cuttings,* Item No. 1, West Bromwich Library.

EPIPHANY: FIRE AND WASSAIL: F. W. Hackwood, 7; C. H. Poole, *The Customs Superstitions and Legends of the County of Stafford,* undated, 15.

CARROLL FOR A WASSELL BOWL: William Hone, *The Everyday Book,* 1827, Vol. II, 10-11; M. and J. Raven, 53.

WALSALL/MOSELEY DOLE: F. W. Hackwood, 7, 8, 9; Book 5, *Newspaper Cuttings* 2, West Bromwich Library.

PLOUGH MONDAY: C. H. Poole, 15; John Sleigh, *History of the Ancient Parish of Leek,* 1883, 217; William Hone, *The Everyday Book,* Vol. 1, 1824, 71-7.

CLOGG ALMANACS: Dr Robert Plot, 10-42, 43; G. T. Lawley, 78, 78A; F. W. Hackwood, 1.

February

COLLOP MONDAY: F. W. Hackwood, *Staffordshire Customs, Superstitions and Folklore,* 1924, 10.

GOODISH TUESDAY: *Notes and Queries,* 2nd series, Vol. V, undated, 209; Book 1, *Newspaper Cuttings,* Item No. 4325, 31/32, West Bromwich Library.

PANCAKE BELL: W. Wells Bladen, 'Notes on the Folklore of North Staffordshire chiefly collected at Stone', *North Staffordshire Field Club Transactions,* Vol. XXXV, 1899-1901, 159; Book 5, *Newspaper Cuttings,* Item No. 1, 1, West Bromwich Library; C. H. Poole, *The Customs, Superstitions and Legends of the County of Stafford,* undated, 17; G. T. Lawley, *Staffordshire Customs, Superstitions and Folklore,* undated, 49A-50, *A Collection of Newspaper Cuttings,* Bilston Library.

PANCAKE BELL RHYMES: BILSTON, WEDNESBURY, WOLVERHAMPTON: G. T. Lawley, 49A, 50; F. W. Hackwood 10.

WEDGEBURY, WILLENHALL: G. T. Lawley, 49A, 50.

SCHOOL HOLIDAY RHYME: W. Wells Bladen, 160; G. T. Lawley, 49A, 50; F. W. Hackwood, 10.

FIRST THREE PANCAKES; SACRED PANCAKE RHYME; ADDING SNOW TO BATTER: F. W. Hackwood, 10.

FIRST PANCAKE: W. Wells Bladen, 160.

MIDDAY MEAL: W. Wells Bladen, 160.

SHROVE TUESDAY MARKS START OF OUTDOOR GAMES: TOP SPINNING, TIP CAT, MARBLES: G. T. Lawley, 49A, 50.

SKIPPING, HOP SCOTCH: F. W. Hackwood, 10.

FOOTBALL BELL: G. T. Lawley, 49A, 50.

FOOTBALL GAMES: G. T. Lawley, 49A, 50, F. W. Hackwood, 10; R. Plant, *The History of Cheadle in Staffordshire*, 1881, 19.

SERVANT LAY ABEDS: G. T. Lawley, 49A, 50.

BARRING OUT: Book 1, *Newspaper Cuttings*, 34; C. H. Poole, 17; F. W. Hackwood, 10.

THROWING AT COCKS: G. T. Lawley, 93A, 94.

March

FIG PIE WAKE: *Notes and Queries*, 2nd Series, Vol. 1, undated, 227; Book 5, *Newspaper Cuttings*, 1, No. 1, West Bromwich Library; F. W. Hackwood, *Staffordshire Customs, Superstitions and Folklore*, 1924, 12.

ROAST VEAL AND CUSTARD: W. Wells Bladen, 'Notes on the Folklore of North Staffordshire, chiefly collected at Stone', *North Staffordshire Field Club Transactions*, Vol. XXXV, 1899-1901, 160; F. W. Hackwood, 12; personal communication Miss E. Randle, Tettenhall, 1976.

FRUMITY; CORN SHEAVES; GREY PEAS AND BACON; SIMNEL CAKES; SIM AND NELL; RAIST BEEF AND LAID; BUTTY COLLIERS; FATHERING MONDAY; LENT RHYME: G. T. Lawley, 47A, 48.

DECORATING CHURCH WITH PALMS: C. H. Poole, *The Customs, Superstitions and Legends of the County of Staffordshire*, undated, 19; F. W. Hackwood, 12; Vol. III, *Newspaper Cuttings*, Items 846-7, 28-9, West Bromwich Library.

PALMS AT TETTENHALL AND BURNING CROSSES: Personal communication, Miss E. Randle, Tettenhall, 1976.
PALMS AS CHARM: C. H. Poole, 19.

April

APRIL FOOLS DAY: G. T. Lawley, *Staffordshire Customs, Superstitions and Folklore*, undated, 53A, 54. *A Collection of Newspaper Articles;* W. Wells Bladen, 'Notes on the Folklore of North Staffordshire, chiefly collected at Stone', *North Staffordshire Field Club Transactions,* Vol. XXXV, 1899-1901, 160.

GOOD FRIDAY: G. T. Lawley, 53A, 54

GARDEN PATCH; SOAP SUDS; OINTMENT TO CURE SORES; BREAD TO FIND DEAD BODY: Vol. 6, *Newspaper Cuttings,* Article hand-initialled B. D. M. and dated 4.4.04, 30/C/D, Wednesbury Library.

HOT CROSS BUNS: Vol. 6, 30, 30A; G. T. Lawley, 53A, 54.

RHYMES ON BUNS: G. T. Lawley, 53A, 54.

CHRIST CHURCH SCHOOL: Personal communication, Mrs K. H. Raven, Tettenhall, 1976.

HOLY BREAD: G. T. Lawley, 53A, 54; Vol. 6, 30, C, D.

GREY PEAS AND BACON: G. T. Lawley, 53A, 54.

PACE EGGING: Vol. 6, 30, 30A.

HALLOWED RINGS: G. T. Lawley, 53A, 54.

EASTER SUN DANCE: G. T. Lawley, 95A, 97; Vol. 6, 30 C/D.

CHURCHES DECORATED WITH BOUGHS ETC.: G. T. Lawley, 95A, 97.

CHURCH DECORATION IN 1976: Personal communication, Miss E. Randle, Tettenhall, 1976.

CLIPPING THE CHURCH: G. T. Lawley, 95A, 97; F. W. Hackwood, *Staffordshire Customs, Superstitions and Folklore*, 1924, 14; Vol. 6, 30A.

ROLLING DOWN GRASSY SLOPES: F. W. Hackwood, 14.

HEAVING: Book 8, *Newspaper Cuttings,* 104, 105, item number 2458, West Bromwich Library; C. H. Poole, *The Customs, Superstitions and Legends of the County of Stafford,* undated, 20; John Sleigh, *History of the Ancient Parish of Leek,* 1883, 217; F. W. Hackwood, 12; Amy Lyons, *Black Country Sketches,* 1901, 44-7; Vol. 6, 30A; G. T. Lawley, 95A, 97; William Hone, *The Everyday Book,* Vol. 1, 1824, 423-5.

'JEWS THEY CRUCIFIED HIM': F. W. Hackwood, 16-20.

ST GEORGE'S COURT: Personal communication, Information Department, Lichfield Guild Hall, October 1973.

May

BLACK COUNTRY COLLIERS; MORRIS DANCING: G. T. Lawley, *Staffordshire Customs, Superstitions and Folklore,* undated, 8, *A Collection of Newspaper Cuttings.*

MAYING AND ERECTION OF MAYPOLE: G. T. Lawley, 8; F. W. Hackwood, *Staffordshire Customs, Superstitions and Folklore,* 1924, 15; C. H. Poole, *The Customs, Superstitions and Legends of the County of Stafford,* undated, 25.

MAYPOLE ERECTION RHYME: G. T. Lawley, 8.

MAYPOLE DANCE RHYME: G. T. Lawley, 8; F. W. Hackwood, 15.

DRINKING WHEY (COLLIERS): G. T. Lawley, 12; F. W. Hackwood, 15.

DECORATION OF PIT FRAMES, CHIMNEY STACKS, ETC.: G. T. Lawley, 12.

DECORATION OF HORSES: W. Wells Bladen, 'Notes on the Folklore of North Staffordshire, chiefly collected at Stone', *North Staffordshire Field Club Transactions,* Vol. XXXV, 1899-1901, 160.

FLOWERS AT UTTOXETER: C. H. Poole, 26.

HOBBY HORSE AND MUMMERS: G. T. Lawley, 8A, the Stafford hobby also took place at Christmas and New Year; F. W. Hackwood, 15; Book, 8, *Newspaper Cuttings,* 104, 105, Item No. 2458, West Bromwich Library; *Stafford Borough Account Books,* W.S.L., SMs 366, S.R.O., D 1323/E/1, William Salt Library, Stafford.

MAY TOAST: G. T. Lawley, 12; F. W. Hackwood, 16.

MAY BOUGHS: F. W. Hackwood, 15.

MAY MARRIAGE: G. T. Lawley, 46, 46A, 47.

MAY DEW: G. T. Lawley, 12A; F. W. Hackwood, 15.

BEATING THE BOUNDS; GOSPEL OAKS; GOSPEL TREES: Book 1, *Newspaper Cuttings,* 31, 32, Item 4325, West Bromwich Library; G. T. Lawley, 99, 99A, 100, 100A; F. W. Hackwood, 21-28; see also Plant, *History of Cheadle;* Shaw, *History of Staffordshire;* Hickes-Smith, *History of Brewood;* Sainder, *History of Shenstone; Wolverhampton Chronicle,* May 1823.

MAYFAIR LEEK: M. A. Miller, *Old Leeke,* Vol. 1, 1900, 35; Personal communication from the librarian, Leek Library (letter), 1976.

OAK APPLE DAY: G. T. Lawley, 17A/18, W. Wells Bladen, 60; F. W. Hackwood, 18-20.

WHITSUN CHURCH DECORATIONS: G. T. Lawley, 12A, 101; F. W. Hackwood, 32; C. H. Poole, 28, 29.

WHITSUN ALE: G. T. Lawley, 16; F. W. Hackwood, 31; C. H. Poole, 28, 29.

WHITSUN DANCE AND SONG, SHOOTING FOR SILVER ARROW: G. T. Lawley, 101.

WHITSUN MORRIS AND MUMMING: F. W. Hackwood, 37-40.

GREENHILL BOWER AND COURT OF ARRAY: William Hone, *The Everyday Book,* Vol. II, 1827, 667; S. Shaw, *History and Antiquities of Staffordshire,* 1798, 316-317; F. W. Hackwood, 34-6; C. H. Poole, 26, 27; personal communication from the Librarian, Lichfield, October 1971. Letter.

WELL DRESSING: Personal communications from Mr Baggerley and Mr Makepeace of Endon, 1971; Personal visit to Endon Well Dressing, May 1972; Official Programme of Endon Well Dressing, May 1972; G. T. Lawley, 46, 46A, 47; Dr Robert Plot, *The Natural History of Staffordshire,* 1686, 8-89; H. H. Prince, *Old West Bromwich,* 1924, 44; R. C. Hope, *Holy Wells: Their Legends and Traditions,* 1893, 151-62.

WELL DRESSING TALE: Ruth L. Tongue, *Forgotten Folk-Tales of the English Counties,* 1970, 87-92, told in 1962 by a Tissington Women's Institute member.

June

MIDSUMMER EVE: WITCHES PARLIAMENT; COLLECTION OF FLOWERS; BONFIRES; PROTECTION AGAINST WITCHCRAFT; SUN WHEELS; FERN SEEDS; WATCHMEN, CORNFIELD PERAMBULATIONS, CROSS-WISE STRAWS; PICKING A DAISY HUSBAND: G. T. Lawley, *Staffordshire Customs, Superstitions and Folklore,* undated, 94A, 107, 108A, 7A, 8, 63A, *A Collection of Newspaper Cuttings,* Bilston Library. See also, F. W. Hackwood, *Staffordshire Customs, Superstitions and Folklore,* 1924, 45.

July

WOLVERHAMPTON FAIR AND PROCESSION: G. T. Lawley, *Staffordshire Customs, Superstitions and Folklore,* undated, 107, 108A, 112, *A Collection of Newspaper Cuttings,* Bilston Library; F. W. Hackwood, *Staffordshire Customs Superstitions and Folklore,* 1924, 100, 101; William Hone, *The Everyday Book,* Vol. II, 1827, 939, 940; See also, S. Shaw, *The History and Antiquities of Staffordshire,* Vol. 2, 1798.

August

TUTBURY COURT OF MINSTRELS AND BULL-RUNNING: S. Shaw, *The History and Antiquities of Staffordshire,* Vol. 1, 1798, 52-5; Dr Robert Plot, *The Natural History of Staffordshire,* 1686, 10-69 to 76; Book 5, *Newspaper Cuttings* 4, West Bromwich Library; F. W. Hackwood, *Staffordshire Customs, Superstitions and Folklore,* 1924, 41-4, M. and J. Raven, *Folklore and Songs of the Black Country,* Vol. 2, 1966, 15-17; C. H. Poole, *The Customs, Superstitions and Legends of the County of Stafford,* undated, 30-3; G. T. Lawley, *Historical Notes Relating to the County of Stafford,* undated, 9, Bilston Library.

ROBIN HOOD AT THE TUTBURY BULL-RUNNING: Book 5, *Newspaper Cuttings,* 29, Note XXIV, West Bromwich Library.

CEREMONIAL DANCE AT BETLEY: *Journal of the Folk Song Society,* Vol. IX, 1960-64, 34, from the collection of E. C. Cawte and A. Helm.

September

ABBOTS BROMLEY HORN DANCE: G. T. Lawley, *Historical Notes Relating to the county of Stafford,* undated, 9; M. A. Rice, *Abbots Bromley,* 1939, 67-99, this section contains photographs of the dance and some of the tunes used for it; *Folk-Lore,* Vol. IV, 1893, 172; *Folk-Lore,* Vol. VII, 1896, 382; *Folk-Lore,* Vol. VIII, 1897, 70; Book 1, *Newspaper Cuttings,* undated, 31-32, item 4325, West Bromwich Library; Dr R. Plot, *Natural History of Staffordshire,* 1686, 10-66; W. Wells Bladen, *Annual Report and Transactions of the North Staffordshire Field Club,* Vol. XLII, 1907/1908, 141-4; M. and J. Raven, *Folklore and Songs of the Black Country,* Vol. 1, 1965, 3, 4; Author's personal visit and observations, 1974; F. W. Hackwood, *Staffordshire Customs, Superstitions and Folklore,* 1924, 5/6 (see also *Staffordshire Curiosities* by the same author); Douglas Kennedy, *English Folk Dancing Today and Yesterday* 1964, 69.

SHERIFF'S RIDE, LICHFIELD: Personal communication from H. Appleyard, Lichfield City Librarian, Letter, 1971; personal communication from Information Department, Lichfield Town Hall, 1971; author's personal visit and observation, 1972; F. W. Hackwood, 27; Book 1, 34, item 4329; S. Shaw, *The History and Antiquities of Staffordshire,* Vol. 1, 1798, 316.

NEWCASTLE WAKES: R. Palmer and J. Raven, *Rigs of the Fair*, 1976, 18-21; personal communication, from D. W. Adams, Reference Librarian, Newcastle under Lyme Library, letter, 1971; Broadside, Newcastle Wakes, Newcastle Library, No. 681250782, undated; also printed in the *Newcastle Guardian*, June 1894; tune, With Wellington We'll Go. Version sung under title of *The Nutting Girl*, by Harry Green of Essex, see F. Hamer, *Green Groves*, 1973: John Sleigh, *History of the Ancient Parish of Leek*, 1883, 217; F. W. Hackwood, 105-7; most local history books contain some information on wakes.
MOCK MAYOR CEREMONY: Joseph Mayer, 'Account of the Ancient Custom of Electing a Mock Mayor in Newcastle-under-Lyme', *Proceedings of the Historical Society of Lancashire and Cheshire*, 1850-51, 126-31; F. W. Hackwood, 163; G. T. Lawley *Staffordshire Customs, Superstitions and Folklore*, undated, 74, *A Collection of Newspaper Cuttings*, Bilston Library.
CRYING THE MARE: G. T. Lawley, 64; F. W. Hackwood, 173; William Hone, *The Everyday Book*, Vol. 2, 1824, 1163.
FURMETY: G. T. Lawley, 64; F. W. Hackwood, 49.

October
HIRING FAIR AT BURTON: F. W. Hackwood, *Staffordshire Customs, Superstitions and Folklore*, 1924, 103.
LEEK HIRING FAIR AND WAKE: Personal communication by Eileen M. White, Librarian at Leek Library, letter, 1976.
HORSE FAIRS AND FESTIVAL OF ST MODWEN: F. W. Hackwood, 102, 103.
HALLOWE'EN: Author's personal observation, October, 1974.

November
SOULING: G. T. Lawley, *Staffordshire Customs, Superstitions and Folklore*, undated 40A, 41, A Collection of Newspaper Cuttings at Bilston Library; C. S. Burne, 'Souling, Clementing and Cattening', in *North Staffordshire Field Club Transactions*, Vol. XLIX, 1914-15, 118-22; M. and J. Raven, *Folklore and Songs of the Black Country*, Vol. 1, 1965, 13, 14; Rev. E. Deacon, 'Some Quaint Customs and Superstitions in North Staffordshire and Elsewhere', *North*

Staffordshire Field Transactions, Vol. 64, 1929, 29, 30; C. H. Poole, *The Customs, Superstitions and Legends of the County of Stafford,* undated, 34, 35; John Sleigh, *History of the Ancient Parish of Leek,* 1883, 217; W. Wells Bladen, 'Notes on the Folklore of North Staffordshire Chiefly Collected at Stone', *North Staffordshire Field Club Transactions,* Vol. XXXV, 1899-1901, 162; F. W. Hackwood, *Staffordshire Customs, Superstitions and Folklore,* 1924, 45, 46; J. Broughton, *Staffordshire Collections,* Cuttings from the *Pottery Gazette,* 1823, 24, 25, 142, Noted down from an old Staffordshire woman in 1824, at William Salt Library, Stafford.

FIRST SOULING SONG: F. W. Hackwood, 45, 46.

SECOND SOULING SONG: Dr S. Jackson Coleman, *Treasury of Folklore – Staffordshire Folklore,* No. 44, Pamphlet, 1955.

LEEK MUMMERS PLAY AND HOBBY: John Sleigh, 217.

LAMBSWOOL: C. S. Burne, 121.

THIRD AND FOURTH SOULING SONGS: J. Broughton, 24, 25, 142.

GUY FAWKES NIGHT: Author's observations.

WOLVERHAMPTON'S 1826 BONFIRE NIGHT: G. T. Lawley, *South Staffordshire Stories,* undated, 7, a collection of Newspaper Cuttings, Bilston Library.

PELTING OF GUY WITH MISSILES: G. T. Lawley, *South Staffordshire Stories,* 7.

CLEMENY: F. W. Hackwood, 46, 47; G. T. Lawley, *Staffordshire Customs, Superstitions and Folklore,* undated, 40A, 41; C. S. Burne, 122 to 128; C. H. Poole, 35, 36, 37; M. and J. Raven, 11, 12; personal communication from Mr W. Hickman of Crewe, letter, 1965.

CLEMENY VERSE: G. T. Lawley, 40A.

CLEMENY AT WALSALL: G. T. Lawley, 40A; C. S. Burne, 127, 128; Vol. 5, *Newspaper Cuttings,* 49, item 405, West Bromwich Library.

BITE APPLE: F. W. Hackwood, 46, 47; M. and J. Raven, 11, 12; C. H. Poole, 35, 36, 37; W. Wells Bladen, 164.

APPLE PARING: F. W. Hackwood, 46, 47.

ST CLEMENT: C. S. Burne, 127.

December

ST THOMAS'S DAY: C. H. Poole, *The Customs, Superstitions and Legends of the County of Stafford,* undated, 37, 38; M. and J. Raven, *Folklore and Songs of the Black Country,* Vol. 1, 1965, 15; G. T. Lawley,

Staffordshire Customs, Superstitions and Folklore, undated, 41, *A Collection of Newspaper Articles,* Bilston Library; Book 5, *Newspaper Cuttings,* 2, West Bromwich Library; R. Plant, *The History of Cheadle,* 1881, 19; F. W. Hackwood, *Staffordshire Customs, Superstitions and Folklore,* 1924, 47; See also Moseley's Dole - S. Shaw, *The History and Antiquities of Staffordshire,* Vol. 2, 1798, 73; F. W. Hackwood, 7, 8.

SPICED ALE AND TOASTED CHEESE: W. Wells Bladen, 'Notes on the Folklore of North Staffordshire, chiefly Collected at Stone', *North Staffordshire Field Club Transactions,* Vol. XXXV, 1899-1901, 164.

FURMETY OR FRUMENTY: G. T. Lawley, 20, 21; F. W. Hackwood, 49.

CHRISTMAS DINNER AT ALDRIDGE: C. H. Poole, 44, 45.

PLUMS AT STAFFORD: C. H. Poole, 44, 45; H. Edwards, of Hoxton, *A Collection of Old English Customs and Curious Bequests and Charities; Extracted from the Reports Made by the Commissioners for Enquiring into Charities in England and Wales,* 1842, 6; Book 5, *Newspaper Cuttings,* 2.

LAMBSWOOL: G. T. Lawley, 44a.

ELDERBERRY WINE AND TREE: G. T. Lawley, 20, 21, 44, Dr R. Plot, *The Natural History of Staffordshire,* 1686, 6-52; F. W. Hackwood, 50.

BREAD BAKED ON CHRISTMAS EVE: G. T. Lawley, 20, 21.

MINCE PIES AND BAD LUCK: W. Wells Bladen, 164.

MINCE PIECE BRINGS HAPPY MONTHS: F. W. Hackwood, 49.

MISTLETOE: F. W. Hackwood, 49; G. T. Lawley, 20, 21.

CHALK LINE: G. T. Lawley, 20, 21; F. W. Hackwood, 50.

STRAWS PLACED CROSSWAYS: F. W. Hackwood, 50.

SUN SHINE THROUGH APPLES: W. Wells Bladen, 166.

DECORATION OF HOME AND CHURCH: W. Wells Bladen, 164; G. T. Lawley, 43a; F. W. Hackwood, 49.

DECORATIONS LEFT TILL TWELFTH NIGHT: Author's personal observation.

REMOVAL OF DECORATIONS AT CANDLEMASS: W. Wells Bladen, 166.

DECORATIONS FED TO CATTLE: W. Wells Bladen, 166.

MISTLETOE AND CHRISTMAS: G. T. Lawley, 20, 21; and 43; F. W. Hackwood, 49.

RINGING IN CHRISTMAS MORNING: G. T. Lawley, 20, 21, and 43; F. W. Hackwood, 50.

SITTING UP: G. T. Lawley, 44.

CHRISTMAS WAITS: G. T. Lawley, 44, 44a, F. W. Hackwood, 48; R. Plant, 20; W. Wells Bladen, 165.

TIMBRIL WAITS: G. T. Lawley, 69, 69A.

FARM ANIMALS: W. Wells Bladen, 164; G. T. Lawley, 44; F. W. Hackwood, 50.

FAIRIES: G. T. Lawley, 44, and 20, 21; F. W. Hackwood, 50.

SWORD DANCE: G. T. Lawley, 20, 21, and 44, 44a.

CHRISTMAS MUMMING: F. W. Hackwood, 54-6; W. Wells Bladen, 167-73; M. and J. Raven, 22-6; M. and J. Raven, *Folklore and Songs of the Black Country*, Vol. 2, 1966, 37-9.

CAROLS: W. Wells Bladen, 167-74; G. T. Lawley, 20, 21, 44a; F. W. Hackwood, 50-2; M. and J. Raven, Vol. 1, 1965, 16-21; Vol. 2, 18-22; M. and J. Raven, Vol. 3, 1967, 49-53; W. Wells Bladen, 166.

WASSAILING: F. W. Hackwood, 49; G. T. Lawley, 20, 21.

ABBOTS BROMLEY HOBBY: G. T. Lawley, 20, 21; see also January notes.

HIRING FAIRS: Rev. E. Deacon, 'Some Quaint Customs and Superstitions in North Staffordshire and Elsewhere', *North Staffordshire Field Club Transactions*, Vol. LXIV, 1929, 159.

BURNING A YULE LOG: G. T. Lawley, 44a.

7 *Local Humour* (pages 145-152)

BISHOP AND KETTLE: G. T. Lawley, *Staffordshire Customs, Superstitions and Folklore*, undated, 40, *A Collection of Newspaper Articles*, Bilston Library.

SOLICITOR'S CLERK TO: Vol. 6 *Newspaper Cuttings*, 1902, 20, West Bromwich Library.

RED HOT SHILLING: F. Grice, *Folk Tales of the West Midlands* 1952, 134-36; see the same book for the story of the Irish Officer and the watch and the Clicking Toad, 107-12, and 116-120 respectively.

WEDNESFIELD WAKE BEEF: G. T. Lawley, 6; G. T. Lawley, 40.

RASHERS OF BACON: G. T. Lawley, 40.

'STRAMSHALL': Vol. 2, *Newspaper Cuttings*, undated, 120 item 711, West Bromwich Library.

'THE STOUTEST': Book 5, *Newspaper Cuttings*, undated, 39 note LIII, West Bromwich Library; G. T. Lawley, 5; F. W. Hackwood, *Staffordshire Customs, Superstitions and Folklore*, 1924, 166; S. Shaw, *The History and Antiquities of Staffordshire*, Vol. 1, 1798, 215.

NARROWDALE MOON: G. T. Lawley, 40.

MARCHINGTON AND WREKIN SAYINGS: G. T. Lawley, 6; G. T. Lawley, 40.

WEEPING CROSS SAYING: G. T. Lawlay, 41; Book 5, 39.

'WOTON': G. T. Lawley, 5; F. W. Hackwood, 165: Book 5, 39; *The Staffordshire Sentinel,* Summer Number, 1910, 60.

RHYME, 'A TUMBLE DOWN': F. W. Hackwood, 166.

RHYME, 'OUR NEW CHURCH': G. T. Lawley, 5.

RHYME, 'CALDON ...': F. W. Hackwood, 167, *The Staffordshire Sentinel,* 60.

RHYME, 'TAMWORTH ... ': *The Staffordshire Sentinel,* 60; F. W. Hackwood, 166.

RHYME, 'WALSALL FOR BANDYLEGS': G. T. Lawley, 5; F. W. Hackwood, 165.

RHYME, SUTTON FOR MUTTON: F. W. Hackwood, 165.

DARLASTON FOLK: G. T. Lawley, 5.

'SUNDAY - HOT MEAT': G. T. Lawley, 5.

'NOTTINGHAM ... ': F. W. Hackwood, 167.

'THERE'S BITTERSCOTE': G. T. Lawley, 5; F. W. Hackwood, 166.

SOME MEN LIKE BILSTON MINES: M. and J. Raven, *Folklore and Songs of the Country,* Vol. 2, 1966, 45.

I LIKE A PREACHER: M. and J. Raven, 33.

CHANNEL TUNNEL: Composed by Keith Stevenson of Bilston, 1965.

8   *The Working Day* (pages 153-169)

GABRIEL'S HOUNDS: Dr R. Plot, *The Natural History of Staffordshire,* 1686, Vol. 1-44; The Hounds are also mentioned in F. W. Hackwood, *Staffordshire Customs, Superstitions and Folklore,* 1924, 146; F. W. Hackwood, *Olden Wednesbury,* 1899, 29; C. H. Poole, *The Customs, Superstitions and Legends of the County of Stafford,* undated, 77, 78; G. T. Lawley, *Staffordshire Customs, Superstitions and Folklore,* undated, 4 and 19, *A Collection of Newspaper Articles,* Bilston Library.

SEVEN WHISTLERS: F. W. Hackwood, *Staffordshire Customs, Superstitions and Folklore,* 1924, 146; C. H. Poole, 78; M. and J. Raven, *Folklore and Songs of the Black Country,* Vol. 1, 1965, 50; M. and J. Raven, Vol. 2, 1966, 40; G. T. Lawley, 4.

CROSS EYED WOMAN, ONE LEGGED MAN, ROBIN ON PUMP, ETC: F. W. Hackwood, 146; M. and J. Raven, Vol. 1, 50.

UNLUCKY TO LET FIRE OUT: Amy Lyons, *Black Country Sketches*, 1901, 19.

TO FIND AN OLD SHOE: G. T. Lawley, 4.

COLLIER'S GUIDE TO SIGNS AND WARNINGS: Amy Lyons, 13; F. W. Hackwood, 146.

MEETING WOMAN AT SUNRISE: G. T. Lawley, 4.

COLLIERS NOT WORKING IN PIT: G. T. Lawley, 4.

STEALING FROM DEAD: G. T. Lawley, 4; M. and J. Raven, Vol. 2, 40.

MORRIS DANCING: F. W. Hackwood, *Olden Wednesbury*, 1899, 31.

'O THE SHILLING': F. W. Hackwood, 31.

'BRAVE COLLIER LADS': J. P. Jones, *Staffordshire Collections*, Book V, *Newspaper Cuttings*, 1883, 166, Wolverhampton Library; M. and J. Raven, Vol. 3, 1967, 16; J. Raven, *Songs of a Changing World*, 1972, 6.

'NAIL STRIKE': M. W. Fletcher, broadside in the Collection of M. W. Fletcher, Netherton: Edward I to Edward VIII, pub. by Dudley Public Libraries, 1946, 1969; M. and J. Raven, Vol. 1, 50; J. Raven, *Songs of a Changing World*, 18.

'JOLLY MACHINE': *Potters Examiner*, 21.12.1844.

'TOMMY NOTE': Bound in cover entitled, Theo Vasmer, *Ballads and Broadsides*, undated 56, Birmingham Library; M. and J. Raven, Vol. 1, 53; K. and J. Raven, *Canal Songs*, 1974, 22, 23.

PUB MUSIC: L. T. C. Rolt, *The Inland Waterways of England*, 1950, 183.

'JOHN WILKINSON': A. N. Palmer, *John Wilkinson and the Old Bersham Iron Works*, 1899, 22, 23; M. and J. Raven, Vol. 3, 1967, 68.

FOOT ALE: Vol. 6, *Newspaper Cuttings*, 19, 20, West Bromwich Library.

'EARLY IN THE MORNING'; 'STOP THAT CLOCK': From the recitation of Mrs E. M. Turner of Wednesbury, collected by Dr John Fletcher of Walsall.

'SONG OF THE STAFFORDSHIRE MEN': F. W. Hackwood, *Glimpses of Bygone Staffordshire*, an undated collection of *Newspaper Cuttings*, Wolverhampton Library; a different version credited to E. M. Rudland appears on a separate printed sheet in Vol. X of *Staffordshire Newspaper Cuttings*, F. W. Hackwood, undated, inserted at page 7, Wolverhampton Library.

'O'D AYNUCK': From the collection of Dr John Fletcher, Walsall, contributed anonymously.

STREET CRIES, WATER CRESS, GET YER SOND, ALL ALIVE, GOOD ODE
MOTHER: From the collection of Dr John Fletcher.
BROOM SELLING AND CRIES: G. T. Lawley, 98a; M. and J. Raven,
Folklore and Songs of the Black Country, Vol. 2, 1966, 26.
MAGIC POOLS, DRUID MERE, HUNGRY POOL, UNNAMED POOL,
MAHALL: G. T. Lawley, *Historical Notes Relating to the County of
Stafford,* undated, 2, 3, Bilston Library.
WALSALL RAIN-MAKER: *Express and Star,* 28.8.76 and 31.8.76.
BARREL ROLLING AT BURTON: *The Guardian,* 4, 28.6.76.

9   *Sports and Pastimes* (pages 170-182)

COCK FIGHTING: William Sketchley, *The Cocker,* 1814, Robert
Howlett, *The Royal Pastime of Cockfighting,* 1709; George Wilson, *The
Commendation of Cockes, and Cockfighting,* 1607, copy British Museum;
Gervase Markham, *The Fighting Cock,* 1615, copy Ohio State
University.
'WEDGEBURY COCKING': Broadside, William Salt Library, Stafford;
Broadside, Local History Collection, Bilston Library.
'WEDNESFIELD WAKE': F. W. Hackwood, *The Annals of Willenhall,*
1908, 188.
COCK-FIGHTING: Vol. 9, *Newspaper Cuttings,* undated, 42, 43, West
Bromwich Library.
BULL BAITING AT STONE: W. Wells Bladen, 'Notes on the Folklore
of North Staffordshire, chiefly collected at Stone', *The Transactions of
the North Staffordshire Field Club,* Vol. XXXV, 1899-1901, 161.
BULL BAITING: Probyn, *A Short Authentic Account of the Late Decision
on the Bull Baiting Problem,* Local History Collection, Birmingham
Reference Library; J. F. Gordon, *Staffordshire Bull Terrier Owner's
Encyclopaedia,* 1967; J. F. Gordon, *Staffordshire Bull Terrier,* 1971.
'THE BLOXWICH WAKE': E. J. Homeshaw, *The Story of Bloxwich,* 1955,
220.
BULL BAITING AT BILSTON: Vol. 9, *Newspaper Cuttings,* 42, 43, West
Bromwich Library.
FRENCH AND ENGLISH: G. T. Lawley, *Staffordshire Customs, Supersti-
tions and Folklore,* undated, 64, *A Collection of Newspaper Articles,*
Bilston Library; F. W. Hackwood, *Staffordshire Customs, Superstitions
and Folklore,* 1924, 20.

MIMIC WARFARE: G. T. Lawley, 67A.

STREET FOOTBALL: G. T. Lawley, *Bilston in the 17th Century,* 1920, 67.

NINE MEN'S MORRIS: G. T. Lawley, 64; F. W. Hackwood, 172.

PRISON BARS: W. Wells Bladen, 161, 162; G. T. Lawley, 65; F. W. Hackwood, 171, 172.

ACCOUNT, PRISON BARS: G. T. Lawley, 65.

TIP CAT: W. Wells Bladen, 161, 162, Joseph Strutt, *The Sports and Pastimes of the People of England,* 1833, 101/102.

DOG STICK; DOG IN THE HOLE; GAME OF DIVINATION: G. T. Lawley, 65.

ROUNDERS: G. T. Lawley, 65; F. W. Hackwood, 173.

TUTBALL: F. W. Hackwood, 173, 174.

CUCKOO OR HIDE AND SEEK: G. T. Lawley, 65; F. W. Hackwood, 170.

STAG WARNING: F. W. Hackwood, 174.

'THE GAME'S BROKE UP': F. W. Hackwood, 174.

Folk Museums

Museums of Staffordshire life are to be found at Burton upon Trent, Dudley, Leek (Cheddleton), Lichfield, Newcastle under Lyme, Stafford, Stoke on Trent (Gladstone Pottery Museum), Shugborough, Tamworth, Walsall, Wednesbury and Wolverhampton (Bantock House).

Bibliography

W. BERESFORD, *Memorials of Old Staffordshire*, 1909

W. WELLS BLADEN, "Folklore of North Staffordshire Chiefly Collected at Stone," in *North Staffordshire Field Club Transactions*, Vol. XXXV, 1899-1901

REV. BRIGHT, *Tale of Ipstones*, 1937

J. BROUGHTON, *Staffordshire Collections*, 1823, 24, 25

C. S. BURNE, *Shropshire Folklore*, 1883

DR. S. JACKSON COLEMAN, *Treasury of Folklore, Staffordshire Folklore*, Number 44, 1955

REV. E. DEACON, "Some Quaint Customs and Superstitions in North Staffordshire and Elsewhere," in *North Staffordshire Field Club Transactions*, Vol. 64, 1929

R. K. DENT, and J. HILL, *Historic Staffordshire*, 1896

J. F. GORDON, *Staffordshire Bull Terrier Owner's Encyclopaedia*, 1967

J. F. GORDON, *Staffordshire Bull Terrier*, 1971

F. GRICE, *Folk Tales of the West Midlands*, 1952

D. R. GUTTERY, *Pensnett and Kingswinford*, 1950

F. W. HACKWOOD, *Staffordshire Customs, Superstitions and Folklore*, 1924.

Sedgley Researches, 1896

Staffordshire Curiosities, 1905

Staffordshire Stories, 1906

Staffordshire Gleanings, 1922

Glimpses of Bygone Staffordshire, circa 1925

Staffordshire Miscellany, 1927

Notes and Queries, Vol. I, II, III, Wednesbury Library, undated.

E. J. HOMESHAW, *The Story of Bloxwich*, 1955

WILLIAM HONE, *The Every Day Book*, Vol. 1, 1824

The Every Day Book, Vol. 2, 1827

R. C. HOPE, *Holy Wells: Their Legends and Traditions*, 1893

J. W. JONES, *History of the Black Country*, undated

D. KENNEDY, *English Folk Dancing Today*, 1964

G. T. LAWLEY, *Staffordshire, Customs, Superstitions and Folklore*, Bilston Library, undated, circa 1922
M. S. Notes and Newspaper Cuttings, Bilston Library, undated
South Staffordshire Stories, Bilston Library, undated
Historical Notes Relating to the County of Stafford, Bilston Library, undated
Bilston in the 19th century, 1920
AMY LYONS, *Black Country Sketches*, 1901
M. A. MILLER, *Old Leeke*, Vol. 1, 1900
A. N. PALMER, *John Wilkinson and the Old Bersham Ironworks*, 1899.
R. Palmer *Songs of the Midlands*, 1972
R. PALMER and J. RAVEN, *Rigs of the Fair*, 1976
W. PAYNE, *Stafford and Its Associations*, 1887
R. PLANT, *History of Cheadle*, 1881
DR. R. PLOT, *The Natural History of Staffordshire*, 1686
C. H. POOLE, *The Customs, Superstitions and Legends of the County of Stafford*, undated, circa 1875
H. H. PRINCE, *Old West Bromwich*, 1924
M. and J. RAVEN, *Folklore and Songs of the Black Country and West Midlands*, Vol. 1, 2, 3, 1965, 66, and 67
J. RAVEN, *Songs of a Changing World*, 1972
M. A. RICE, *Abbots Bromley*, 1939
S. SHAW, *History and Antiquities of Staffordshire*, 2 Vols., 1798
J. SLEIGH, *History of the Ancient Parish of Leek*, 1883
P. TRAVIS, *In Search of the Supernatural*, 1975
R . TONGUE, *Forgotten Folk Tales of the English Counties*, 1970
E. A. UNDERHILL, *Story of the Ancient Manor of Sedgley*, 1941

In addition, the following newspaper cutting volumes were consulted:

J. P. JONES, *Staffordshire Collections*, 1883, Wolverhampton Library
Staffordshire Sentinel, Summer Numbers, 1909, 1910, Stoke on Trent Library
Book 1, Vol. 2, Vol. 3, Book 5, Vol. 6, Vol. 8, Vol. 9, *Newspaper Cuttings*, West Bromwich Library

Index of Tale Types

Folktales are named and classified on an international system based on their plots devised by Antti Aarne and Stith Thompson in *The Types of the Folktale*, 1961; numbers from this system are preceded by the letters AT. Local legends were partly classified by R. Th. Christiansen in *The Migratory Legends*, 1958; his system was further developed by K. M. Briggs in *A Dictionary of British Folktales*, 1970-1. These numbers are preceded by ML, and the latter are also given an asterisk.

Motif Index

Motifs, which are elements recurring within the plot of one or several folktales (e.g. 'cruel stepmother' in both 'Snow White' and 'Cinderella'), have been classified thematically in Stith Thompson's *Motif Index of Folk Literature*, 1966, and in E. Baughman's *Type and Motif Index of the Folktales of England and North America*, 1966.

General Index